PRAISE FOR
SHIFTING ATMOSPHERES

Two things have become priorities for me in life and ministry: making sure we (the Bethel family) are living by the principles of the Kingdom of God and are giving ourselves to caring for and valuing the atmosphere of the King. At the end of the day, it's all about the presence of God and His purposes in our lives. That's why I'm so happy about this book, *Shifting Atmospheres*. Author Dawna De Silva does a great job of instructing us how to change the atmosphere in any situation. She is a trusted voice in our environment here at Bethel Church. She speaks and writes with great authority and insight because this is how she lives. I strongly recommend this wonderful book, as it will equip you with insight, inspiration, and the courage needed to profoundly impact the world you live in.

BILL JOHNSON
Bethel Church, Redding, CA
Author of *God is Good*

I have known Dawna De Silva for many years and it's been an honor to watch her step into her calling and teach others to shift spiritual atmospheres. Her new book, *Shifting Atmospheres*, sheds light on the spiritual realm in a way that is clear and easy to understand. I believe that the revelation in this book will dispel any fear that you may have when approaching the mysteries of the unseen realm. Using Jesus as the ultimate role model and biblical foundation of truth, Dawna will empower you to take authority over spiritual atmospheres through discernment, gaining insight, and using Kingdom weapons like peace, joy, and worship. I highly recommend this book to anyone who operates in the gift of discernment and wants to live an empowered, victorious, and free life!

KRIS VALLOTTON
Leader, Bethel Church, Redding, CA
Co-founder of Bethel School of Supernatural Ministry
Author of eleven books including
The Supernatural Ways of Royalty and *Spirit Wars*

There is a very real spirit world all around us. Just beyond the veil of what we can see with natural eyes, there is a realm that's even more real than what we can experience with our senses.

We as Christians should not be ignorant of this realm. It's a realm where angels and demons dwell, and this realm lives among us. For many believers, this world of the spirit remains invisible to the natural senses. Some are given opportunities to catch glimpses of how this unseen realm operates. For most, it remains invisible, but just because it's invisible doesn't mean it doesn't have influence and impact.

I believe the Lord is raising up voices that remind the Body of Christ that this spiritual realm is very real, very present among us, and a very real source of conflict. And yet, these voices don't just point to the activities of darkness—they provide strategies for how you and I, people filled with the Holy Spirit, can and should establish the spiritual atmospheres around us.

Dawna De Silva understands much about this realm. In her book *Shifting Atmospheres*, she does an excellent job of breaking it down and giving us behind-the-scenes understanding into this realm. She explains how we can operate in *victorious* spiritual warfare and stand in our God-given right to take authority over the spiritual atmospheres for our families, homes, and cities.

BENI JOHNSON
Bethel Church
Best-selling author of *The Happy Intercessor, Healthy and Free,*
and *40 Days to Wholeness*

There is a current flurry of activity in the ministries of deliverance and inner healing that arguably has not been seen since the Jesus Movement of the 1970s. I believe the Lord is bringing this ministry back to the forefront.

Hosea 4:6 says that people perish or are destroyed for lack of knowledge. The church has been wandering in the wilderness in this area of ministry for much too long. It's time to see God's people set free.

Dawna's new book unpacks the weapons of our warfare, which are indeed mighty in God for pulling down strongholds. She does it in a simple and realistic way.

Be informed and be equipped. I highly recommend this work.

DR. WILLIAM (BILL) SUDDUTH
President, International Society of Deliverance Ministers

In her book *Shifting Atmospheres,* Dawna De Silva provides refreshing insight into the realms and dimensions of the spirit while equipping the reader to conquer the attacks of the enemy. Just when I thought there was not another creative way to write about spiritual warfare, Dawna surprised me and beautifully articulated Kingdom truths on this vital subject. I am passionate about the education of believers in the area of spiritual warfare and personal freedom; that is why I am excited about this book!

RYAN LESTRANGE
Founder, Tribe Network/Ryan LeStrange Ministries
Author, *Overcoming Spiritual Attack* and *Supernatural Access*

I just read Dawna De Silva's new book, *Shifting Atmospheres,* and I have one word that can describe it—*balanced!* It takes on one of the toughest subjects and injects some spiritual intelligence as well as some well-thought-out reworking of some very touchy subjects. If we are going to shift atmospheres in culture, we have to have tools like this to give us a modern understanding while not sacrificing the power of the Gospel. This book will be quoted by many in the future and has set a new benchmark in our focus on both the strategy of the enemy but ultimately our focus on Jesus and His Kingdom that never ends.

SHAWN BOLZ
TV Host and author of *God Secrets, Translating God,*
and *Keys to Heaven's Economy*
www.bolzministries.com

At a time when many wear rose-colored glasses and pretend that the devil doesn't exist, Dawna De Silva gives a refreshing reminder: True victory isn't in the denial of evil, but it's in the defeat of evil. In *Shifting Atmospheres,* she carefully uncovers the realities of our enemy and his tactics. But she doesn't dwell there. Instead, Dawna passionately focuses on Christ and reveals step by step how to activate an atmosphere of His power over yourself, your home, and your region. Truly, *Shifting Atmospheres* is a profound resource that moves you from the trappings of fighting a devil who's defeated to living in the victory of the One who defeated him.

KYLE WINKLER
Author of *Activating the Power of God's Word*
and creator of the Shut Up, Devil! app
www.kylewinkler.org

Dawna De Silva has written a book that is necessary for *all* in the Body of Christ. *Shifting Atmospheres* is a unique, excellent resource to help every believer understand how to activate faith to impact the environments around them. Faith is believing when not seeing. Faith works in time and space. Dawna has an incredible ability to capture how to see into your time and space to discern your atmosphere and to see what you can't see. I believe this book will break the "Thomas Syndrome" off the Body of Christ. Thomas had to see to believe. *Shifting Atmospheres* explains how to see the invisible around you. These are days when the atmospheres of Heaven and earth are aligning. This book is a must for now!

Dr. Chuck D. Pierce
Best-selling author of *Worship Warrior, Protecting Your Home from Spiritual Darkness,* and *A Time to Triumph*
President, Global Spheres Inc.
President, Glory of Zion Intl.

God has given us authority to heal the sick, cast out devils, raise the dead—and shift atmospheres. Often, we sense with our spirits what we don't see with our eyes, and we can shift it with Spirit-led words in the name of Jesus and spiritual weapons like peace, home, and worship.

In *Shifting Atmospheres*, Dawna De Silva teaches us how to discern spiritual atmospheres everywhere we go so we can release the Kingdom and dispel powers of darkness for God's glory. With scriptural backing and practical examples, Dawna inspires us to partner with Holy Spirit to boldly take authority over demon powers that defy the will of God in our lives, our homes, and our cities. I highly recommend this book to Christ-centered spiritual warriors!

Jennifer LeClaire
Senior Editor of *Charisma Magazine*
Best-selling author of *Waging Prophetic Warfare* and *The Spiritual Warrior's Guide to Defeating Jezebel*

SHIFTING
ATMOSPHERES

DESTINY IMAGE BOOKS BY DAWNA DE SILVA

Sozo: Saved, Healed, Delivered (with Teresa Liebscher)

SHIFTING ATMOSPHERES

DISCERNING & DISPLACING
THE SPIRITUAL FORCES
AROUND YOU

DAWNA DE SILVA

DESTINY IMAGE® PUBLISHERS, INC.

P.O. Box 310, Shippensburg, PA 17257-0310

"Promoting Inspired Lives."

This book and all other Destiny Image and Destiny Image Fiction books are available at Christian bookstores and distributors worldwide.

Cover design by Eileen Rockwell
Interior design by Terry Clifton

For more information on foreign distributors, call 717-532-3040.

Reach us on the Internet: www.destinyimage.com.

ISBN 13 TP: 978-0-7684-1566-7
ISBN 13 eBook: 978-0-7684-1571-1
ISBN 13 HC: 978-0-7684-1646-6
ISBN 13 LP: 978-0-7684-1647-3

For Worldwide Distribution, Printed in the U.S.A.

1 2 3 4 5 6 7 8 / 21 20 19 18 17

I dedicate this book to the warriors in God's Kingdom:
those who have gone before,
those who are still fighting today,
and those who will carry the seeds of freedom into the future.

ACKNOWLEDGMENTS

This book would never have made it to the press without my son, Cory, lifting the heaviest weights. I am so grateful for his time and energy spent researching, outlining, and creating endless rough drafts for me to revise.

Thanks also to my good friend, Susan Anderson, for her insight on shifting atmospheres through hope and peace as well as her numerous read-throughs during our flights this past year.

I also want to thank Stuart Gregg for his valuable scriptural insight and probably missing a few of his dear *Dr. Who* episodes to help us make our deadline.

I thank my husband, Stephen, profusely for allowing me to use some of his personal revelations in this book—a true benefit of "one flesh."

And thanks to all my friends, family, and Sozo peeps around the world who have been faithful to walk this path with me in learning how to discern, describe, and shift atmospheres.

CONTENTS

INTRODUCTION

For we do not wrestle against flesh and blood, but
against the rulers, against the authorities, against
the cosmic powers over this present darkness, against
the spiritual forces of evil in the heavenly places.
—Ephesians 6:12

Whether we like it or not, we humans have been born into a war, one that pits darkness against light—Satan, the accuser of the brethren, against God the Most High (see Rev. 12:10). While Scripture makes it clear this battle is unevenly matched, we sons and daughters of the King still find ourselves in the enemy's crosshairs from time to time. In his book *The Three Battlegrounds*, author Francis Frangipane writes, "Some of us may never actually initiate spiritual warfare but all of us must face the fact that the devil has initiated a war against us."[1] As followers of Christ, it is important that we acknowledge the sovereignty of God but also accept the fact that Satan has launched a violent campaign against us.

Each of us has experienced occasional sickness, discouragement, and other unexplained phenomena. While I do not think every issue we face is caused by demons, I do want to open your eyes to the fact that there is an enemy out there focused on bringing you to destruction.

Succeeding in spiritual warfare does not solely come through acknowledging its presence. We must take possession of the truths presented in Scripture and arm ourselves like valiant warriors. The Bible says, "My people are destroyed for lack of knowledge" (Hos. 4:6). God wants us to be educated so we can defend ourselves against the lofty ideas Satan raises up against the will of God (see 2 Cor. 10:5).

When we are ignorant of the enemy's designs, we leave ourselves open to attack. Knowing this, we must prepare ourselves for spiritual battle so that we are not sideswiped by the enemy. This, however, does not mean we steward an unhealthy obsession with the demonic, for that is not helpful in any way. Instead, we must keep our eyes focused on God and wield strength from His perspective. As we focus on Christ, we discover His heavenly strategies and learn how to implement them to destroy the devil's plans.

As a deliverance minister for over twenty years, I have witnessed God bring personal and corporate breakthrough to tens of thousands of believers. Though spiritual warfare can seem intense, those committed to Christ are more than over-comers. I encourage you to study this book and read each chapter presented. Your victory—whether gaining new ground, resisting the enemy, or receiving a long-desired healing—might be just one page away.

> *You are the light of the world. A city set on a hill cannot be hidden. Nor do people light a lamp and put it under a basket, but on a stand, and it gives light to all in the house. In the same way, let your light shine before others, so that they may see your good works and give glory to your Father who is in heaven* (Matthew 5:14-16).

NOTE

1. Francis Frangipane, *The Three Battlegrounds* (Cedar Rapids, IA: Arrow Publications, 2006).

CHAPTER ONE

THE SPIRITUAL REALM

*For by him all things were created, in heaven
and on earth, visible and invisible, whether
thrones or dominions or rulers or authorities—all
things were created through him and for him.*
—COLOSSIANS 1:16

t was about three in the afternoon when the demon first
appeared. My oldest son, Cory, stood in the living room,
shocked. This shaded figure, as real as any stranger standing on
a street corner, stood silent and watching. Cory backed away
and asked Holy Spirit what was going on.

This is a demon that represents an assignment against you, the Holy Spirit said. *Its job is to make sure you do not fulfill your destiny in Los Angeles.*

Filled with the Holy Spirit, Cory took stock of the phantom and strode up like a gunslinger out of The Good, The Bad, and The Ugly. He declared, "Get out in Jesus's name!"

Without lingering, the spirit vanished. My son looked about the room—in awe of his own spiritual authority.

Many believers are surprised to find that issues they face are caused by demonic activity. Be it a sickness or financial crisis, partnership with sin, or an outright attack, believers can be just as harassed by demons as non-believers. While I do not believe Christians can be possessed (because the Holy Spirit lives inside us), I do believe unclean spirits can attach themselves to us in various ways. I do not say this to imply the devil carries more power than Christ inside of us. Again, there is no equal to God. However, when Christians lack the tools necessary for identifying and rejecting the devil's schemes, they leave themselves open to demonic influence and attack.

Many Christians have no idea how much the spiritual realm affects their health, thought processes, or daily lives. Demonic forces of various levels vie for control. These cohabiters of earth, bound to the unseen realm, include rulers, authorities, dominions, principalities, and powers (see Eph. 6:12). As followers of Christ, our job is to reduce and remove the impact of these evil beings and replace their influence with God's Kingdom.

The first step to becoming victorious in the spiritual realm is to admit it exists. Jim Daly from Focus on the Family writes:

There is a lack of understanding about the spiritual realm and the influence that it has on the physical realm. The spiritual precedes, influences and, to many degrees, determines the physical realm. The better we understand the spiritual and how it relates to the physical, the better we are able to operate as Christians.[1]

Humanity is made in God's image. However wrecked or broken we may be, we still reflect our Creator. God is Spirit, so we too are spiritual beings (see John 4:24). We are not just flesh and blood. A biblical Hebraic reading of Scripture makes it clear that we humans share biological, physiological, and spiritual realities. We are more than just skin and emotions.

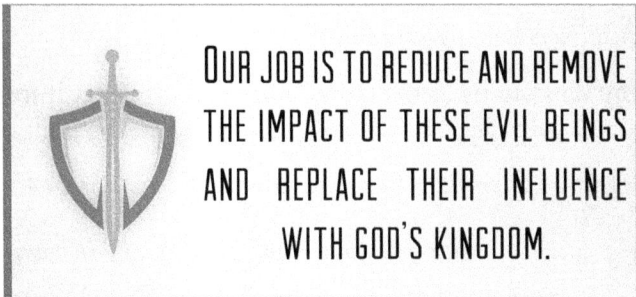

> OUR JOB IS TO REDUCE AND REMOVE THE IMPACT OF THESE EVIL BEINGS AND REPLACE THEIR INFLUENCE WITH GOD'S KINGDOM.

Just as God spoke and the light came into being, we physical beings have an anchoring in the spirit. This is why Christ tells us:

Do not lay up for yourselves treasures on earth, where moth and rust destroy and where thieves break in and steal, but lay up for yourselves treasures in heaven, where neither moth nor rust destroys and where thieves do not break in and steal. For where your treasure is, there your heart will be also (Matthew 6:19-21).

Christ encourages us to keep our citizenship in heaven—for that is where our redeemed selves truly reside (see Eph. 2:6). We must realize that although we experience a period of time on earth, our physical lives possess eternal purpose.

To see our families, communities, and cities brought back to the Lord, we need to recognize that the spiritual realm is very much at work. We have an enemy who recognizes this and does his best to take advantage of our lack of understanding. Denial is a prolific way for us to avoid truth. Yet at some point in our denial, reality intervenes and leaves us in a state of shock wondering, *where did that come from?*

Many Christians (especially those in Western culture) place a greater emphasis on the physical—things that can be seen or proven. But as Scripture says, the invisible realm is just as real.

> *You worship what you do not know; we worship what we know, for salvation is from the Jews. But the hour is coming, and is now here, when the true worshipers will worship the Father in spirit and truth, for the Father is seeking such people to worship him. God is spirit, and those who worship him must worship in spirit and truth* (John 4:22-24).

Contemporary culture seems obsessed with all things related to the spiritual. Books and movies featuring ghosts, monsters, and other supernatural beings stock the shelves of libraries, stores, and other virtual markets worldwide. Entertainment's vampires, werewolves, and masked killers are examples of how we humans long to explore realities we cannot fully explain. These mythical monsters and the evil they embody mimic a spiritual truth—we struggle not against flesh and blood but against the spiritual beings. Although we cannot see them, they exist and seek to influence our physical realm.

I believe people are drawn to stories about monsters because we have an innate need for justice. Most audiences want to see the bad guy lose, the good guy win, and the monsters defeated. This need is a reflection of God's nature in us because He is the ultimate representation of justice. We are designed to destroy the works of evil. Our weapons, however, are not hate, jealousy, or outrage. They are, instead, spiritual weapons revealed in Scripture that enable us to stand in the truth of who we are in Christ.

God has called us to become beacons of light so we can draw people to Christ and release them from bondage. For too long, Christians have been asleep at the gates—unaware their own souls are oppressed by the demonic. It is time for us to partner with God and help shift the atmospheres of this world to what He originally intended. As we fulfill our calling to be the salt of the earth, we will stop the enemy's broadcasts (lies spoken over a region) and present ourselves as partners of the earth's transformation.

The idea that Satan poses a threat to God is ill-educated at best. The Bible states, *"To whom then will you compare me, that I should be like him? says the Holy One"* (Isa. 40:25). There is not and will never be an equal to the Almighty God. Any attempts to raise up Satan as an equal opponent are lies fabricated by the enemy.

Although Satan possessed authority over the earth subsequent to Adam and Eve's sin, Jesus's resurrection reinstated His and man's authority over the earth. When Jesus ascended into heaven, He declared, *"All authority in heaven and on earth has been given to me"* (Matt. 28:18). He then commissioned His followers to go and make disciples of all nations, saying, *"I am with you always, to the end of the age"* (Matt. 28:19-20).

If Jesus has been given all authority and commissioned us with that same power, why then does it seem at times like the world is overtaking us rather than us overtaking the world?

Although Jesus has been given *all* authority, Satan still desires to disrupt God's purposes for mankind. Satan's army of demons, principalities, powers, world rulers, and deceived humans works to carry out the devil's ungodly schemes of separation and condemnation. Examples of the enemy's schemes abound—divided societies, the poor being forgotten, the rich hated, marriages failing, and perversion being both championed and celebrated. Our role is to fight these corrupting influences—not by engaging in warfare with our neighbors, spouses, or coworkers, but through bringing God's goodness, love, and truth to the situation.

Although there are times when physical warfare is justified, our enemies are not the people themselves but the spiritual forces who advise and rule over them.

Through the Holy Spirit in us, we can take back Satan's occupied land and release God's presence in its place. By exercising our God-given spiritual authority, we can confront the works of the enemy and follow the example of Christ who defeated evil through His love and sacrifice.

It is time to take up our swords of the Spirit and drive back Satan's armies. In these days when violence is promoted, the sex trade booms, and morality fades, the church must stand up, expose evil, and release truth. As we fulfill our assignment as co-laborers with Christ, we unleash more opportunities to secure God's Kingdom on earth. This has been our calling since the beginning and is the worldwide mission of shifting atmospheres:

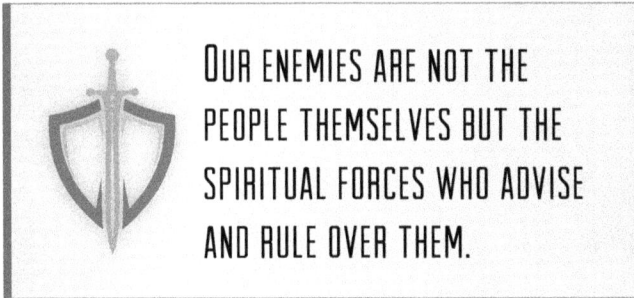

> OUR ENEMIES ARE NOT THE PEOPLE THEMSELVES BUT THE SPIRITUAL FORCES WHO ADVISE AND RULE OVER THEM.

For the creation waits with eager longing for the revealing of the sons of God. For the creation was subjected to futility, not willingly, but because of him who subjected it, in hope that the creation itself will be set free from its bondage to corruption and obtain the freedom of the glory of the children of God (Romans 8:19-21).

NOTE

1. Jim Daly, "The Reality of Spiritual Warfare," Billy Graham Evangelistic Association, January 24, 2005, https://billygraham.org/decision-magazine/february-2005/the-reality-of%20spiritual-warfare/.

CHAPTER TWO

SPIRITUAL STRATEGIES

*Finally, be strong in the Lord and in the strength of
his might. Put on the whole armor of God, that you
may be able to stand against the schemes of the devil.*
—EPHESIANS 6:10-11

M an is made up of body, soul, and spirit. It should not
surprise us that the enemy attacks us in all three areas (see
Eph. 6:16). Sometimes, his arrows hit us in our actual bodies
and result in sickness or disease. Other times, his arrows
target our minds and result in confusion or mental torment.

Least understood is how hell's fiery arrows affect our spirits. I have found that we need spiritual strategies to protect each of these areas.

Psalm 103:3-4 tells us that God pardons *"all your iniquity"* (the sins of your soul), heals *"all your diseases"* (the effects on your body), and redeems *"your life from the pit"* (the effects on your spirit). Teresa Liebscher's and my inner healing ministry, Sozo, is built on these truths. Coming from the Greek word *sōzō*, which is used one hundred times in the New Testament, the ministry provides God's promise of being "saved, healed, and delivered." It denotes a whole package—not just physical healing but also emotional and spiritual wholeness.

When our bodies are targeted by the enemy's fiery arrows, prayers of healing are employed to make them well:

> *Is anyone among you sick? Then he must call for the elders of the church and they are to pray over him, anointing him with oil in the name of the Lord; and the prayer offered in faith will restore the one who is sick, and the Lord will raise him up, and if he has committed sins, they will be forgiven him. Therefore, confess your sins to one another, and pray for one another so that you may be healed* (James 5:14-16 NASB).

This verse, although referencing physical sickness, also contains insight into links between the body (sickness) and the soul (sin). I have found many times that physical healing follows inner healing. Once our sins are confessed, lies uprooted, and truth revealed, physical healing can naturally occur. More than any other aspect of our physical being, our mind dictates the realities by which we live. This is why Scripture tells us to "renew our minds" (see Rom. 12:2).

The devil and his forces feed off immorality and spiritual darkness. This darkness grows as our minds partner with *lies* (deceptions). These are Satan's fiery arrows, which are used to distract us from the Lord's truth. This is at the forefront of all spiritual warfare and is covered by Joyce Meyer in her book *The Battlefield of the Mind*. In it, she identifies the mind as the part of a human being most assaulted.

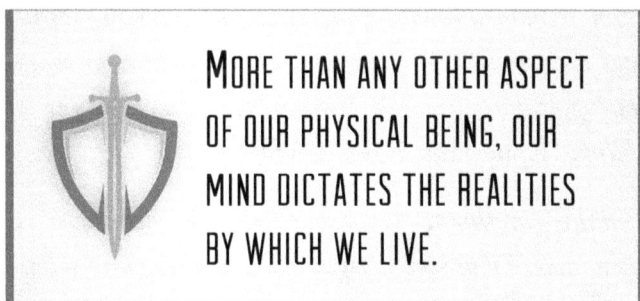

> **MORE THAN ANY OTHER ASPECT OF OUR PHYSICAL BEING, OUR MIND DICTATES THE REALITIES BY WHICH WE LIVE.**

> Satan's target [is] your mind. [His] weapons [are] lies. [His] purpose [is] to make you ignorant of God's will. Your defense? The inspired Word of God.[1]

Without the Word of God showing us His truth, our *truths* (or what we perceive to be true) will govern our minds. A great book that explores thought processes and how they transform into actions is Dr. Carolyn Leaf's *Who Switched off My Brain?* In it, she coins the phrase "toxic thoughts." This is a great metaphor for how Satan tries to get us to believe lies about ourselves and others.

If we are to be powerful, influential believers, we need to have authority over our mind. This happens by identifying and rejecting those thoughts that are not from God and then replacing them with His truths. Our starting point for this is in Psalms, Ephesians, and Philippians:

> *I will set no worthless thing before my eyes; I hate the work of those who fall away, it shall not fasten its grip on me* (Psalm 101:3 NASB).

> *But immorality or any impurity or greed must not even be named among you, as is proper among saints; and there must be no filthiness and silly talk, or coarse jesting, which are not fitting, but rather giving of thanks* (Ephesians 5:3-4 NASB).

> *Finally, brethren, whatever is true, whatever is honorable, whatever is right, whatever is pure, whatever is lovely, whatever is of good repute, if there is any excellence and if anything worthy of praise, dwell on these things* (Philippians 4:8 NASB).

You can easily recognize thoughts or lies from the enemy because they lead you away from the Person of Jesus. If a thought or impression comes from God, it will always bring you closer to Him and His virtues.

One of our strongest techniques for warfare is to ground ourselves in Scripture. Jesus demonstrated this when He was tempted by the devil in the wilderness. This living and breathing Word not only provided Him with truth but ultimately protected Him from the devil's schemes. Scripture works the same way for us. When we are assaulted by lies and deceptions, God's Word is our first reliable source of rebuttal:

> *For the word of God is living and active, sharper than any two-edged sword, piercing to the division of soul and of spirit, of joints and of marrow, and discerning the thoughts and intentions of the heart* (Hebrews 4:12).

If we are to live empowered, influential lives, we need to reinforce our minds with Scripture. Paul calls the Word of God our sword of the Spirit (see Eph. 6:17). Interestingly, it is our only weapon listed in that famous passage. Sadly, many Christians (especially in the West) go into battle unequipped and without their swords.

According to one survey conducted by the Barna Group for the American Bible Society, "Only 26 percent of Americans said they read their Bible on a regular basis (four or more times a week)." When applying this study to young people, a "majority (57 percent) of those ages 18-28 read their Bibles less than three times a year, if at all."[2]

This study reveals how the majority of Americans are unequipped to do any kind of spiritual battle. Without their swords, they are unable to rightly decide between truth and error. Given the percentages in this survey, it is no surprise to see the United States has drifted from a foundation of Christian values to one of secularism and humanism.

Perhaps one of the biggest reasons we find ourselves under spiritual attack is because we fail to prepare ourselves for battle.

As the saying goes, "By failing to prepare, you prepare to fail." By failing to spend time in God's Word, we ignore the most important blueprint He has laid out for our lives. Likewise, when we deny a personal relationship with the Holy Spirit, we distance ourselves from the very Person who is able to guide us through all circumstances. The Bible states:

> But the Helper, the Holy Spirit, whom the Father will send in my name, he will teach you all things and bring to your remembrance all that I have said to you (John 14:26).

To be effective in spiritual warfare requires partnership with God's Spirit and His Word.

Spiritual attacks are a direct assault from the demonic realm and gain influence as more and more people practice and tolerate sin. This sin creates *open doors* that allow the demonic more access into a person's life. As more and more people steward evil, demons are drawn to their body, region, or territory. Francis Frangipane writes:

> If we *tolerate* darkness through tolerance of sin, we leave ourselves vulnerable to Satanic assault. For wherever there is willful disobedience to the Word of God, there is spiritual darkness and the potential for demonic activity.[3]

Jesus warns of what happens when individuals practice sin:

> Truly, truly, I say to you, everyone who practices sin is a slave to sin (John 8:34).

When people propagate partnerships with sin, ungodly atmospheres spread. Soon entire cities and regions become spiritual cesspools from which the devil's armies can operate.

***

Perhaps one of the best ways we can learn to excel in spiritual warfare is to study the life of Jesus. More than any other person in Scripture, Jesus demonstrated how to live in power and humility. It is important to examine His ministry so we can determine how to best go about succeeding in the spiritual realm and warfare.

Jesus did not just come to grant salvation—though that would have been enough for us to be eternally grateful. He also came to demonstrate powerful living. During Jesus's time on earth, He depicted God's Kingdom on the earth. This resulted in the departure of sickness, disease, and torment. At the end of His ministry, He gave His life willingly so God's Kingdom could be fully established. Tom Wright, the British theologian, described Christ's death as the following:

> The early Christians believed that something happened on the cross itself, something of earth-shattering meaning and implication, something as a result of which the world was now a different place. A revolution had been launched.[4]

The King had been enthroned, although not in the way anyone had expected. Jesus displayed through both His life and death that the Kingdom of God was not just about saving souls but also about bringing the goodness of God into every aspect of life.

With spiritual warfare, much of our success comes from simply displaying the goodness of God. Love, heaven's greatest weapon, covers a multitude of sins; when released, it can crush the enemy's forces no matter how strong.

The arrival of Jesus, love personified, changed everything. He replaced the temple and became the arena in which sin could be forgiven and humans could have direct communication with God (see Mark 2:5; John 14:9). He declared that the exiles were forgiven and could return to live under the Father's blessing (see Luke 15). In His life, Jesus overthrew the impacts of sin and the effects of Satan's kingdom.

In His death, every sickness, disease, and torment became an illegal offense that we today have the authority to renounce. As we continue to bring our struggles before the Father, our mediator, Jesus, stands by our side and silences the accuser (see 1 John 2:1). Thanks to Jesus, a new world order has been established—one with Him at the center. We must continue to cultivate what He has started.

———✠———

I believe the primary reason for Jesus's success in His ministry was His steadfast devotion to His Father. The Bible says the two were so connected there was nothing Jesus could do that was not a part of His Father's will:

> So Jesus said to them, "Truly, truly, I say to you, the Son can do nothing of his own accord, but only what he sees the Father doing. For whatever the Father does, that the Son does likewise" (John 5:19).

We even see this connection developing as a child. When Mary and Joseph left Jesus behind in Jerusalem, they found Him days later conversing with the temple's teachers. When asked why He had disappeared, Jesus responded:

Why were you looking for me? Did you not know that I must be in my Father's house? (Luke 2:49)

Shortly after, Scripture says, *"Jesus increased in wisdom and in stature and in favor with God and man"* (Luke 2:52). If Jesus had to increase in favor with God and man, how much do we need to grow?

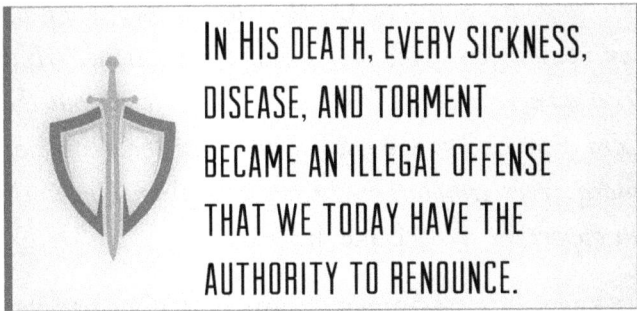

> IN HIS DEATH, EVERY SICKNESS, DISEASE, AND TORMENT BECAME AN ILLEGAL OFFENSE THAT WE TODAY HAVE THE AUTHORITY TO RENOUNCE.

Protecting and cultivating such a strong connection to God is important and allowed Jesus to mature in His gifts and to grow in authority. His authority grew to become so palpable that demons would cry out for mercy whenever He approached:

And demons also came out of many, crying, "You are the Son of God!" But he rebuked them and would not allow them to speak, because they knew that he was the Christ (Luke 4:41).

Jesus, the ultimate servant, surrendered Himself to God fully. This resulted in some of the most miraculous signs and wonders experienced in human history.

As mentioned earlier, some of Jesus's success was also attributed to His understanding of Scripture. During His time in the wilderness with Satan, Jesus used the Word of God to cut down the devil's lofty arguments:

> *And he took him to Jerusalem and set him on the pinnacle of the temple and said to him, "If you are the Son of God, throw yourself down from here, for it is written, 'He will command his angels concerning you, to guard you,' and 'On their hands they will bear you up, lest you strike your foot against a stone.'" And Jesus answered him, "It is said, 'You shall not put the Lord your God to the test.'" And when the devil had ended every temptation, he departed from him until an opportune time* (Luke 4:9-13).

Jesus knew His assignment from the Father had yet to be completed, so He must have known that hurling Himself from the temple would result in angels coming to His rescue. Rather than conform to the devil's taunts, Jesus stayed the path God set for Him and parried Satan's use of Scripture with His own.

Sometimes, the devil uses what we know or what we think we know to try and weaken us. It is important to remember that he is a liar. It should not surprise us, then, how he twists everything to try and bait us away from the Father's will. To combat his distractions, we must dig deep into the Word of God. In it is our proper footing from which we dare not stray.

Another major reason for Jesus's success was His reliance on the Holy Spirit. Jesus made clear how much value He placed on the Holy Spirit:

> *Therefore I tell you, every sin and blasphemy will be forgiven people, but the blasphemy against the Spirit will not be forgiven. And whoever speaks a word against the Son of Man will be forgiven, but whoever speaks against the Holy Spirit will not be forgiven, either in this age or in the age to come* (Matthew 12:31-32).

Jesus so prized this connection that He was willing to put forth the ultimate boundary. If anyone uttered even a word against the Spirit, Jesus asserted they would never be forgiven. Theologians debate whether this sin is truly unforgivable. Regardless of what you believe, it is important to see how fiercely Jesus protected His connection.

Not only did Jesus's partnership with the Holy Spirit result in signs and wonders, it also enabled Him to operate with a strong discernment. With this gift, Jesus deciphered thoughts, spirits, and people's internal struggles. Because of this, He was able to escape dangerous and manipulative scenarios:

> *But Jesus, aware of their malice, said, "Why put me to the test, you hypocrites? Show me the coin for the tax." And they brought him a denarius. And Jesus said to them, "Whose likeness and inscription is this?" They said, "Caesar's." Then he said to them, "Therefore*

render to Caesar the things that are Caesar's, and to God the things that are God's." When they heard it, they marveled. And they left him and went away (Matthew 22:18-22).

He also used His gift to distinguish evil spirits and teach people how to best drive them out:

And when he [Jesus] had entered the house, his disciples asked him privately, "Why could we not cast it out?" And he said to them, "This kind cannot be driven out by anything but prayer" (Mark 9:28-29).

Lastly, Jesus's gift enabled Him to detect hidden agendas even in those closest to Him. In His exchange with Peter, Jesus discerned the devil's veiled intentions:

But he turned and said to Peter, "Get behind me, Satan! You are a hindrance to me. For you are not setting your mind on the things of God, but on the things of man" (Matthew 16:23).

Those wounded by suspicion, bitterness, and jealousy sometimes are critical of discernment because they have felt condemned or judged by it in the past. A true gift of discernment, however, is rooted in love. The apostle John wrote:

There is no fear in love, but perfect love casts out fear. For fear has to do with punishment, and whoever fears has not been perfected in love (1 John 4:18).

If there is anything other than love motivating your discernment, repent and ask for God's forgiveness. He does not take the abuse of His gifts lightly but is always willing to extend grace to those who repent:

If we confess our sins, he is faithful and just to forgive us our sins and to cleanse us from all unrighteousness (1 John 1:9).

Timing is yet another principle Jesus mastered. Content to operate on His Father's time frame, Jesus spent the first thirty years of His life living what many would consider to be a normal existence. During this time, Jesus stewarded His identity, grew in His understanding of culture, and increased in favor by both stewarding and fulfilling the assignments God gave Him.

So many of us run headlong into ministry without taking the time to develop our character or favor. This can lead to us to be sidelined by discouragement, impatience, and our lack of preparedness. It is important to know Jesus took the time to prepare Himself for God's calling. He did not simply wait around for thirty years. He stewarded the life God had given Him.

We can also examine how Jesus took the time to withdraw from crowds when needed (see Luke 5:16). Spiritual discipline, prayer, and fasting are vital foundations for growing a strong connection with the Father. Bill Johnson says, "If Jesus did what He did as the perfect Son of God then I am impressed, but I can never do what He did. If Jesus did what He did from a life of obedience and His in-filling with the Holy Spirit, then I am given the model for how I am to live."[5]

Content with waiting thirty years (the majority of His life), Jesus served as a perfect sign of obedience. Doing so laid the groundwork for His ministry and the redemption of millions.

Once He was anointed, the unstoppable influence of heaven was activated.

> SO MANY OF US RUN HEADLONG INTO MINISTRY WITHOUT TAKING THE TIME TO DEVELOP OUR CHARACTER OR FAVOR.

We can learn endless lessons from Jesus's life. As we, too, wait on God's promises, it is important we do not forsake His timing. Remember, Satan wanted Jesus to take his shortcut in the wilderness. The temptations that Satan offered were very specific and targeted the very mission Jesus had come to accomplish. Jesus was offered a kingdom, but not the Kingdom. He was offered power without submission—authority that is grasped, not given. While doing so may have prevented His painful death on the cross, Jesus knew doing things God's way would redeem mankind and lead us to freedom:

> *Though* [Christ Jesus] *was in the form of God,* [he] *did not count equality with God a thing to be grasped, but emptied himself, by taking the form of a servant, being born in the likeness of men. And being found in human form, he humbled himself by becoming obedient to the point of death, even death on a cross. Therefore God has highly exalted him and bestowed on him the name that is above every name, so that at the name of Jesus every knee should bow, in heaven and on earth and under the earth, and every tongue confess that*

Jesus Christ is Lord, to the glory of God the Father (Philippians 2:6-11).

NOTES

1. Joyce Meyer, *Battlefield of the Mind* (New York: Faith Words, 2002), 11-12.

2. Caleb Bell, "Americans Love the Bible but Don't Read It Much, Poll Shows," The Huffington Post, April 04, 2013, http://www.huffingtonpost.com/2013/04/04/americans -love-the-bible-but-dont-read-it-much_n_3018425.html.

3. Francis Frangipane, "Satan's Domain: The Realm of Darkness," Ministries of Francis Frangipane, August 2015, https://francisfrangipanemessages.blogspot.com/2015/08/satans-domain-realm-of-darkness.html.

4. N.T. Wright, *The Day the Revolution Began* (San Francisco, CA: HarperOne, 2016), 169.

5. Bill Johnson, "As He Is, So Are We." Bethel.TV, 4 Nov 2012, http://www.bethel.tv/watch/1485/as-he-is -so-are-we/2012/11/04.

CHAPTER THREE

TACTICS OF THE ENEMY

There are two equal and opposite errors into
which our race can fall about the devils. One is
to disbelieve in their existence. The other is to
believe, and to feel an excessive and unhealthy
interest in them. They themselves [the devils]
are equally pleased by both errors and hail a
materialist or a magician with the same delight.
—C.S. LEWIS, *The Screwtape Letters*

In order to disrupt the church's understanding of spiritual warfare, the devil has put forth several ideological errors to distort truth. As mentioned by C.S. Lewis, the first of these, *post-enlightenment rationalism*, denies that anything exists beyond what can be seen, touched, or explained. This is the primary mindset of Western society where a high value is placed on the material while the spiritual world is left largely unexplored.

A second error, and equally destructive, is the embrace of an unhealthy obsession with the demonic. This puts Christians and non-Christians alike in an unfortunate place of focus. The devil becomes "bigger" in their eyes as they fixate on an inferior kingdom. While partnering with these mindsets manifests in different ways, both have their origins in deception.

As Paul instructs, we are called to keep our focus on God. We acknowledge the presence of an enemy but never allow its existence to overshadow our reverence of Him. As Paul writes, whatever we focus on is what we become:

> *If then you have been raised with Christ, seek the things that are above, where Christ is, seated at the right hand of God. Set your minds on things that are above, not on things that are on earth. For you have died, and your life is hidden with Christ in God* (Colossians 3:1-3).

The devil does not care what we believe so long as it hinders our relationship with God. Both denial of the spiritual realm and an unhealthy obsession with it lead to distraction. As we ping-pong from one extreme to the other, we lose sight of truth. Soon our time is filled with either cultic obsession or blind, spiritual ignorance.

I encounter these two extremes often through my travels across the globe. I find churches either believe *everything is a demon* or deny the enemy is at work altogether. When churches focus too much on the enemy, undercurrents of fear and suspicion spread throughout their congregations. Churches that remain ignorant of the spiritual realm corrode internally as their blind leaders stand by unaware of the underlying spiritual attacks.

My husband, Stephen, author of *Money and the Prosperous Soul*, describes the pull of the two extremes this way, "The enemy does not care which side of the horse you fall off on. He just wants you off the horse." Satan always wants attention, however skewed it may be. It does not matter how he gets it so long as he keeps our focus on his realm rather than on God's. To obsess over the demonic realm gives it unnecessary power and fosters paranoia. Soon we begin "worshiping" what the devil is doing to us rather than what God wants to do through and for us.

———✦———

Years ago, I attended prayer meetings filled with fun, rowdy intercessors. Determined to scare off the forces of evil with our authority, we stomped our feet, waved our arms, blew shofars, and shouted aggressively while commanding all the unclean spirits to leave. Although I usually left these sessions feeling empowered, I was confused that shortly thereafter I found myself facing the exact same issues as before.

In the long run, these experiences actually left me discouraged and perplexed at our apparent lack of authority. As I spoke with more prayer warriors, it seemed our only strategy was to fight harder, longer, and louder. Fortunately, I have learned a lot since then in my understanding of the spirit realm.

Contrary to this rowdy type of warfare is a complete denial of all things spiritual. These are the saints who embrace God's Word but disregard His Spirit. Ignorance is not bliss because it disconnects them from receiving guidance from their Helper and therefore blinds them to the actual war going on around them.

When spiritual attacks do come, ignorant saints feel side-swiped. Expecting no danger whatsoever, they blame others for the harm they are experiencing and retaliate against spouses, friends, and co-workers instead of the spiritual forces driving them. Eventually, they can even begin to blame God for not protecting them from these seemingly surprise attacks; they forgot that *"we do not wrestle against flesh and blood"* (Eph. 6:12).

Christians commit spiritual suicide by lacking a healthy perspective on spiritual warfare. They either slip into *everything is bad* and search for demons behind every bush or embrace an ignorant mindset and offer themselves up as easy targets. Neither of these outlooks leads to spiritual health. We either focus on God's goodness and strength or fall prey to the devil's schemes.

In *The Happy Intercessor*, Beni Johnson highlights the importance of focusing on God's perspective. Even when picking up on (seeing/sensing) what is going on in the spiritual realm, she describes how important it is to find God's heartbeat. This allows us to discover how He sees a situation and what He wishes to impart. If our cities are steeped in darkness, it is our responsibility to partner with Him and release His opposite (see 1 John 1:5).

> CHRISTIANS COMMIT SPIRITUAL
> SUICIDE BY LACKING A
> HEALTHY PERSPECTIVE ON
> SPIRITUAL WARFARE.

To have a healthy outlook on spiritual warfare, we need to understand the Bible's stance on the subject. If we look at Ephesians 6:12 without the surrounding verses for context, we can easily be pulled into the extreme perspective of exhausting warfare. Balancing this verse with the others shown below gives us a proper perspective of our authority.

> *For we do not wrestle against flesh and blood, but against the rulers, against the authorities, against the cosmic powers over this present darkness, against the spiritual forces of evil in the heavenly places* (Ephesians 6:12).

> *I do not cease to give thanks for you, remembering you in my prayers, that the God of our Lord Jesus Christ, the Father of glory, may give you the Spirit of wisdom and of revelation in the knowledge of him, having the eyes of your hearts enlightened, that you may know what is the hope to which he has called you, what are the riches of his glorious inheritance in the saints, and what is the immeasurable greatness of his power toward us who believe, according to the working of his*

great might that he worked in Christ when he raised him from the dead and seated him at his right hand in the heavenly places, **far above all rule and authority and power and dominion,** *and above every name that is named, not only in this age but also in the one to come* (Ephesians 1:16-21).

But God, being rich in mercy, because of the great love with which he loved us, even when we were dead in our trespasses, made us alive together with Christ— by grace you have been saved—and raised us up with him and seated us with him in the heavenly places in Christ Jesus (Ephesians 2:4-6).

When we line these verses up together, we see God's balance of truth. Though we are in a real war, we are seated with Christ in the heavenly places. This is a position high above every rule, authority, power, and dominion. Knowing this, there is no reason we should be afraid.

So many Christians live in fear when in reality hell cowers at the Spirit of God within them. The Bible says creation waits for the sons and daughters of God to be revealed (see Rom. 8:19). When we figure out who we are and whose we are, we become Christlike—an unstoppable force that batters the enemy's ranks. It is important to realize how frequently the enemy uses fear as a tactic. A traveling preacher told a story about this while preaching at Bethel.

> THOUGH WE ARE IN A REAL WAR, WE ARE SEATED WITH CHRIST IN THE HEAVENLY PLACES. KNOWING THIS, THERE IS NO REASON WE SHOULD BE AFRAID.

Years ago, he was on a ministry trip with his longtime friend and mentor, Bob Jones. During the first night, Bob woke up to see a very large demon standing at the foot of his bed. He commanded it to leave and went back to sleep only to be awakened later by the same spirit. Instead of partnering with fear, Bob said, "Oh, it's just you. Go bother Larry." The unclean spirit vanished and Bob enjoyed the rest of his night. The next morning, Bob ran into Larry downstairs—who appeared quite exhausted. When he told Bob he had wrestled throughout the night with a demon, Bob simply informed him, "I know. I sent him to you."

While this may seem cruel, Bob used this as a lesson to teach Larry something important. The enemy feeds off fear. Larry could have renounced partnership with it and sent the demon away. Instead, he gave in to fear and this allowed the unclean spirit to harass him throughout the night.

Often, demons appear to us in frightening ways (or forms they think will frighten us). This is why some people believe in ghosts and haunted houses. These phantoms are not ghosts but demons who have taken up residence to spread fear. All the "ghost hunter" shows on TV could be solved with one visit by a confident, Spirit-filled believer on assignment from God.

Renouncing partnership with fear is one of the quickest ways to disarm demonic attacks. This does not mean the harassment ends instantly; "resisting the devil" implies more than just saying "no" (see James 4:7; Eph. 6:13-14; Ps. 91). When we know who we are and who is covering us, we can stand firm in the midst of any spiritual assault.

Several years ago while on a ministry trip to England, I experienced a targeted harassment. During one of my first nights there, I woke up with an overwhelming urge to go out and buy pornography. Knowing this was an attack (I never normally have this urge), I got out of bed prayed and worshiped until this drive left me. I knew my inner self was pure to sexual sin, so this attack, which was obviously sent from a spirit of perversion, could not bait me. Because of my confidence in who I "normally was" (how I acted, thought, and felt on a normal basis), I easily identified this as an attack from the enemy and used this realization to stand firm and not give in to buying pornography. Instead of buckling under the assault, I submitted myself to God through worship and prayer:

> *Submit yourselves therefore to God. Resist the devil, and he will flee from you* (James 4:7).

One of the biggest ways the devil infiltrates our lives is through the practice of sin. If he can get us to partner with any aspect of it, ungodly doors will be opened into our lives and allow evil spirits access. I believe this is what God is warning us of in the following verse:

Be angry and do not sin; do not let the sun go down on your anger, and give no opportunity to the devil (Ephesians 4:26-27).

In the original Greek, *opportunity* translates as either a *place, opportunity, portion,* or *space.* According to this verse, by sinning we create a spiritual territory the devil can access.

Jesus knew the danger of partnering with sin, so He upped the ante during His ministry on the earth. Whereas the Old Testament commanded us to not commit adultery, Jesus taught not to even look with lust at a woman. Throughout His teachings, Jesus set a "higher bar" for us to follow. He emphasized the "you have heard it said, but now I say to you" gospel. The good news is He also equipped us with the ability to fulfill these higher callings.

While temptation itself is not sin, the actions resulting from it are. Bethel's inner healing ministry, Sozo, examines open doors in people's lives to see whether they are partnering with sin. These four doors are *fear, hatred/bitterness, sexual sin,* and *dealings with the occult.* Sozo ministers check each category and facilitate sessions so that clients can repent from sin and restore their relationship with the Father.

The Bible makes it clear that sin hinders communication with God. Although He is willing to reach out and redeem those who are lost, when we practice sin it muddies and sometimes blocks free and personal communication with Him:

We know that God does not listen to sinners, but if anyone is a worshiper of God and does his will, God listens to him (John 9:31).

When dealing with someone who has an open door, Sozo-ers partner with the Holy Spirit to help clients work through a process of repentance, renunciation, forgiveness, and acceptance of God's truth. Each door covers broad categories and houses a myriad of other related sins.

According to the *Four Doors* tool, behind the door of fear exists *worry, unbelief, need for control, anxiety, isolation, apathy, drugs,* and *alcohol addictions.* Behind hatred/bitterness is *bitterness, envy, gossip, slander, anger,* and *self-hatred (low self-worth).* In sexual sin is *adultery, pornography, fornication, lewdness, molestation, perversion, fantasy,* and *rape.* The last door, the occult, includes *astrology, fortune-telling, tarot cards, séances, Ouija boards, manipulation, control, participation in covens, casting curses,* and other *witchcraft practices.*

Some of these doors may be hard for Christians to investigate. For instance, not many people want to admit they struggle with hatred or bitterness, let alone culture-shaming issues like pornography. Some of these areas are painful to investigate, but it is important for the person's health that they bring these issues before the Father.

Other terms used to describe open doors are *hooks* or *pockets of darkness.* The meaning is the same regardless of how you choose to identify them. Make sure any areas of your life that you feel are in partnership with sin are renounced and forgiven by Christ. Leaving something to fester will only lead to imprisonment. I have witnessed such breakthrough in people's lives as they bring their sin to light, renounce participation with it, and receive Christ's forgiveness.

Any part of our lives not submitted to the blood of Christ has the potential to house demonic activity. The devil and his minions exist in areas of spiritual darkness, so any areas in our lives not surrendered to God have the potential to invite the demonic. Whether these holds on your life speak to you as *doors*, *hooks*, or *areas of darkness*, make sure you take ownership over yourself and bring any issues before God. Doing so will eradicate the devil's footholds and set you up for success in spiritual warfare.

Perhaps the most common tactic the enemy uses against us is *lying*. In fact, this is the first tactic the devil used to deceive Eve in the Garden. This tactic is how the devil uses deception to trick us into believing in falsehoods. When we agree with these unhealthy mindsets, we partner with sin and act out of our old, dead natures. We resurrect our old humanity and give it power to dictate our actions. The apostle Paul writes:

> *So you also must consider yourselves dead to sin and alive to God in Christ Jesus* (Romans 6:11).

Paul tells us to *consider* (or add up or come to the logical conclusion) ourselves dead to sin and new creations in God's redemptive and restorative power. When we give our lives to Christ, we receive a new mind. Paul even goes so far as to tell us we are given the *"mind of Christ"* (1 Cor. 2:16). How then can so many Christians hear the enemy's voice and backslide into sin? The answer is deception. The devil is a master of deceit and has been so from the beginning. In Genesis, the serpent's words were:

> *Did God actually say, "You shall not eat of any tree in the garden"?* (Genesis 3:1)

This was a direct challenge to God's command just moments before and was almost the exact opposite of what the Lord actually told Adam and Eve.

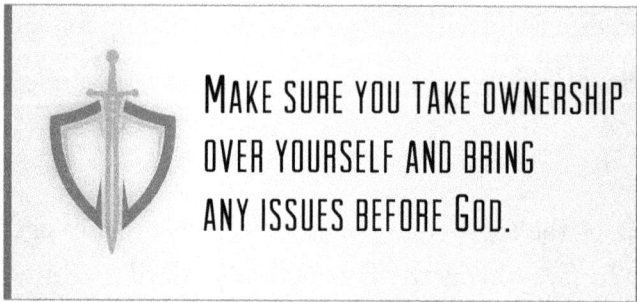

MAKE SURE YOU TAKE OWNERSHIP OVER YOURSELF AND BRING ANY ISSUES BEFORE GOD.

Although we are given the mind of Christ, we are not given an invisible force field set up to ward off all of the enemy's schemes. This is why Paul encourages us to put on and wear the full armor of God. While the shield of faith extinguishes the enemy's arrows, our helmet of salvation, our breastplate of righteousness, our belt of truth, and our sandals of peace will protect us from any accurate missiles.

Lies are the primary way evil spirits communicate with us. By tricking us into believing their mindsets, demons get us to partner with their schemes. This then creates behavioral patterns that result in action. As we agree with these agendas over time, warped mindsets develop. This is how strongholds form. Years of agreeing with lies like *I am unworthy* or *I am stupid* create cyclical patterns that manifest physically in the form of addictions, sins, and destructive life patterns. Soon we are acting against God's original design for our lives.

These lies typically exist at a subconscious level, sometimes stewarded from the time of birth or early childhood. Having such ideologies ingrained from a young age, people are often unable to identify their presence. Taking the time to allow the Holy Spirit to point out any ungodly mindsets helps individuals to ferret out lies and exchange them for the Lord's truth. Until this exchange happens, the person will not be able to fully receive healing.

This minefield of the mind is where the enemy sabotages us. It is why Paul writes in Second Corinthians:

> For though we walk in the flesh, we are not waging war according to the flesh. For our weapons of our warfare are not of the flesh but have divine power to destroy strongholds. We destroy arguments and every lofty opinion raised against the knowledge of God, and take every thought captive to obey Christ (2 Corinthians 10:3-5).

These flaming arrows thrown at your mind must not be partnered with. We must free ourselves from the lies we believe and walk free from the devil's deception.

The Bible defines these lies as arguments and lofty opinions. Some translations even use the word *imaginations*. This is why Paul admonishes us to take every thought captive. The devil wants to plant his lies deep into the soil of our subconscious. Doing this ingrains his false mentalities that, unless uprooted, develop into destructive mindsets.

It is amazing how many Christians fail to seize and take every thought captive because they fail to realize that not all the voices speaking to them are their own. These thoughts just might be whispers of deception coming from evil spirits, which must be renounced.

Be careful to test your thoughts and feelings throughout your day. If you struggle to discern what is from God and what is not, write down what you hear. When God is speaking, even when He confronts us, we will feel His character of love coming through. If you ever find yourself confused in your ability to discern whose voice is talking, remember that anything that does not lead you closer to Jesus is from another kingdom:

> *Beloved, do not believe every spirit, but test the spirits to see whether they are from God, for many false prophets have gone out into the world* (1 John 4:1).

CHAPTER FOUR

WEAPONS OF WARFARE

*For the weapons of our warfare are not of the flesh
but have divine power to destroy strongholds. We
destroy arguments and every lofty opinion raised
against the knowledge of God, and take every thought
captive to obey Christ, being ready to punish every
disobedience, when your obedience is complete.*
—2 CORINTHIANS 10:4-6

The Bible provides a storehouse of weapons for us to use in
spiritual warfare. Apart from what we have already discussed
(*spiritual armor, discernment, and God's Word*), weapons like

worship/praise, prophetic declarations, prayer, tongues, the fruits of the Spirit, and encouraging one's self in the Lord all help us to defend and/or take ground from the enemy. The Bible tells us Jesus has *all* authority. Therefore, we can be confident that His love will cover us as we progress through our learning of spiritual battle.

One of the greatest weapons in our arsenal is worship/praise. When using this technique, we quell the enemy's attempts to infiltrate our minds and hearts. We focus on our original assignment (relationship with God) and deflect the devil's attacks.

Human beings are designed to worship. We see this all throughout history. When humans choose not to worship God, they replace this need with other forms of worship. The Israelites in the wilderness proved this point by worshiping a golden calf after Moses had departed (see Exod. 32:1). I find that when we are not worshiping God wholly, we begin to worship other things—ourselves, relationships, fame, money, possessions, or any other natural or abstract desire. Worship is core to man's nature, and we must aim it at God alone.

> # ONE OF THE GREATEST WEAPONS IN OUR ARSENAL IS WORSHIP.

One night while on a trip, my friend Susan experienced a demonic attack. Sound asleep, I felt God's prompting to wake up and protect her. I turned to ask if she was okay and felt an evil presence standing at the foot of her bed.

"Are you alright?" I asked.

"No," she said. "There's a demon telling me all sorts of lies and I'm struggling to not give in to them."

As I sat up to confront the demon, my head started to spin. Feeling like I was about to vomit, I laid back down. Still trying to wake, I had difficulty not drifting back to sleep. Again, the Holy Spirit prompted me to wake.

As I rose, I began to softly sing, "Who is like unto Thee?" The vertigo loosened its grip as I continued to sit up. I next declared, "Oh Lord among the gods, who is like unto Thee?" My stomach churned, but I continued to sit up and sing even louder until I ended on, "Glorious in Holiness. Fearful in praises and doing wonders. Who is like unto Thee?" As I finished the song, the atmosphere lifted. The demon, frightened by my worship, vanished. The feeling of torment shifted to peace and we both fell fast asleep.

God takes the subject of worship so seriously that He incorporated it into many of His warfare strategies. In Second Chronicles, we saw this demonstrated during the reign of Jehoshaphat:

> *And when he [Jehoshaphat] had taken counsel with the people, he appointed those who were to sing to the Lord and praise him in holy attire, as they went before*

the army, and say, "Give thanks to the Lord, for his steadfast love endures forever" (2 Chronicles 20:21).

Placing musicians on the front lines, Jehoshaphat magnified God's praise. Though a risk, he took the time to create an atmosphere of praise and experienced one of Judah's most miraculous deliverances:

> *And when they began to sing and praise, the Lord set an ambush against the men of Ammon, Moab, and Mount Seir, who had come against Judah, so that they were routed. For the men of Ammon and Moab rose against the inhabitants of Mount Seir, devoting them to destruction, and when they had made an end of the inhabitants of Seir, they all helped to destroy one another* (2 Chronicles 20:22-23).

In this passage, praise confused the enemy. Sent out as a disruptive signal, worship confounded the enemy's ranks and destroyed them so completely that the armies of Judah spent three days collecting spoil:

> *When Jehoshaphat and his people came to take their spoil, they found among them, in great numbers, goods, clothing, and precious things, which they took for themselves until they could carry no more. They were three days in taking the spoil, it was so much* (2 Chronicles 20:25).

If you find yourself in the midst of an impossible situation, worship may be your greatest weapon. In the midst of discouragement, praise can be the very thing that brings you into tomorrow's blessing. Habakkuk depicts this beautifully at the close of his book. During a time of crisis for his people,

Habakkuk exercised faith and praised the Lord for the blessings he had not yet seen:

> *Though the fig tree should not blossom, nor fruit be on the vines, the produce of the olive fail and the fields yield no food...yet I will rejoice in the Lord; I will take joy in the God of my salvation. God, the Lord, is my strength; he makes my feet like the deer's; he makes me tread on my high places* (Habakkuk 3:17-20).

This prophetic foresight displays the creative power of praise. Sometimes worshiping God in the midst of our trials actually creates the breakthrough we are looking for.

This mixes well with one of the other weapons God has placed in our arsenal—prophetic declarations. This is a helpful tool that allows us to seize God's promises that may feel distant or out of reach. In times of warfare, it is imperative we cry out and proclaim God's truths over us. It is a weapon even Job reflected on during his time of difficulty:

> *You will decide on a matter, and it will be established for you, and light will shine on your ways* (Job 22:28).

When we prophetically partner with God's promises (those that have been declared but not yet realized), it creates in us the capacity to receive hope. This is the act of faith Jesus described to His disciples:

> *Whatever you ask in my name, this I will do, that the Father may be glorified in the Son. If you ask me anything in my name, I will do it* (John 14:13-14).

Jesus Himself made prophetic declarations. In Mark 4, Jesus imparted peace to the storm. His inner reality became the atmosphere by which everything else shifted. The result was an instant calm and a pervading fear of God's glory.

> # WHEN WE PROPHETICALLY PARTNER WITH GOD'S PROMISES, IT CREATES IN US THE CAPACITY TO RECEIVE HOPE.

Last year, I took a stroll through my neighborhood. It was after the third year of a drought, and most of the lawns had died due to lack of water. The lawns had turned yellow, and it seemed the neighbors' motivation to keep them pretty had died as well. Staring at the mummified remains, I thought, *Well, there goes the neighborhood.*

I heard the Lord say, "It can, but it's up to you."

I thought for a minute and replied, "Lord, I don't have time to paint the outside of my neighbor's house, fix their roof, or water their lawn."

His only answer was, "You know how to do this. You do teach this stuff."

From then on, I declared life into the neighborhood—*this home will be repainted, this roof will be fixed, this lawn will be watered.* When I got home that night, the lawn across from my house was being lavishly watered. It was the first time in months the sprinklers had been on.

By declaring God's opposite (life and beauty), the spiritual atmosphere of dryness shifted. Eventually, the drought ended. Now there is an array of green lawns and refreshed homes dotting our cul-de-sac.

Returning to Jehoshaphat's story, we see another powerful weapon of warfare—prayer and fasting. In Daniel's case, it led to many visions and revelations being imparted. For Jesus, it led to thousands of documented signs and wonders. In Jehoshaphat's case, prayer and fasting led his kingdom to an astonishing victory:

> *Some men came and told Jehoshaphat, "A great multitude is coming against you from Edom, from beyond the sea; and, behold, they are in Hazazon-tamar"* (that is, Engedi). *Then Jehoshaphat was afraid and set his face to seek the Lord, and proclaimed a fast throughout all Judah. And Judah assembled to seek help from the Lord; from all the cities of Judah they came to seek the Lord* (2 Chronicles 20:2-4).

> *And the Spirit of the Lord came upon Jahaziel the son of Zechariah...in the midst of the assembly. And he said, "Listen, all Judah and inhabitants of Jerusalem and King Jehoshaphat: Thus says the Lord to you, 'Do not be afraid and do not be dismayed at this great horde, for the battle is not yours but God's* (2 Chronicles 20:14-15).

The lesson to glean from this is the power of bringing our feelings, problems, and situations before the Lord. As a loving and perfect Father, He is never ashamed of our thoughts or issues, He simply wants to deliver us. As Stephen De Silva says, "God is a deliverer by nature. It is not *if* He will deliver us but *when*."[1]

Prayer is powerful. It helps us gain God's perspectives and receive His strategies. Although we will discuss intercessory prayer in the last chapter, for now realize prayer's importance and work to improve its frequency in your life. Three wonderful messages you can listen to on prayer are Stephen De Silva's "Shirtless in My Offering"[2] and "Praying It Forward"[3] and my message entitled "Praying from Power."[4]

> AS A LOVING AND PERFECT FATHER, HE IS NEVER ASHAMED OF OUR THOUGHTS OR ISSUES, HE SIMPLY WANTS TO DELIVER US.

The gift of tongues is an effective yet sometimes frowned upon weapon for spiritual warfare. It is sometimes seen as a time-specific gift, but it nevertheless serves as an important form of prayer. While I do not wish to argue points of theology, below are some Scriptures that support its use:

> *Pursue love, and earnestly desire the spiritual gifts, especially that you may prophesy. For one who speaks in a tongue speaks not to men but to God; for no one*

understands him, but he utters mysteries in the Spirit. On the other hand, the one who prophesies speaks to people for their upbuilding and encouragement and consolation. The one who speaks in a tongue builds up himself, but the one who prophesies builds up the church (1 Corinthians 14:1-4).

Translations for the phrase *builds up* include "to build a house, erect a building, to build (up from the foundation), to restore by building, to repair, found, establish, to promote growth in Christian wisdom, affection, holiness." While Paul states prophecy is used to grow the church in wisdom, grace, and holiness, tongues is the private form of communication between a person and the Lord. This is why Paul encourages us to learn how to translate tongues. If we do so, it makes the individual blessing corporate:

Therefore, one who speaks in a tongue should pray that he may interpret. For if I pray in a tongue, my spirit prays but my mind is unfruitful. What am I to do? I will pray with my spirit, but I will pray with my mind also; I will sing praise with my spirit, but I will sing with my mind also. Otherwise, if you give thanks with your spirit, how can anyone in the position of an outsider say "Amen" to your thanksgiving when he does not know what you are saying? For you may be giving thanks well enough, but the other person is not being built up (1 Corinthians 14:13-17).

Whether you use this gift for your own spiritual growth or translate it for your church's community, be sure to keep Jesus as the forefront. Spiritual gifts, especially tongues, can cause offense because they are culturally and societally foreign.

In the Book of Acts, the apostles' use of tongues caused such a commotion that thousands were saved but many were held back due to offense:

> *And all were amazed and perplexed, saying to one another, "What does this mean?" But others mocking said, "They are filled with new wine"* (Acts 2:12-13).

The key to moving past offense is to examine a gift's fruit. If it moves people closer to Jesus, then it is from God. Jesus spoke about examining fruit throughout His ministry to help His followers navigate false doctrine. In Matthew, He encouraged His followers:

> *Beware of false prophets, who come to you in sheep's clothing but inwardly are ravenous wolves. You will recognize them by their fruits. Are grapes gathered from thornbushes, or figs from thistles? So, every healthy tree bears good fruit, but the diseased tree bears bad fruit* (Matthew 7:15-17).

If you find yourself uncomfortable with a gift or ministry, use discernment to examine its fruit. Be careful, however, not to let your own personal biases skew your judgment.

Sometimes our personal fears and viewpoints warp our opinions. Though some moves of God cause discomfort, the resulting fruits should always lead people closer to Jesus. Peter confronted peoples' fears about tongues in Acts when he encouraged them that this demonstration was the result of an outpouring of God. Following his message, thousands were saved.

Often when God prompts me to pray, I naturally slip into my prayer language. I find that this helps to disconnect my mind from trying to solve the problem myself and prepares me to hear the Lord's solution. The gifts of the Spirit should never be separate from the fruits of the Spirit. Galatians 5:22-23 says:

> But the fruit of the Spirit is love, joy, peace, patience, kindness, goodness, faithfulness, gentleness, self-control; against such things there is no law.

Just because the fruits and the gifts of the Spirit are listed in separate letters does not mean we should keep them apart. We assess the gifts of the Spirit by their fruit. If a tongue or prophecy does not lead to deeper love, joy, peace, or any of the other fruits, then we should be cautious in accepting its practice. If it does, then we should not hesitate to incorporate it into our lives.

Another potent weapon of warfare—and arguably one of our most effective—is God's Word. Described as the Sword of the Spirit, Scripture is one of our most devastating tools to use against the enemy:

> For the word of God is living and active, sharper than any two-edged sword, piercing to the division of soul and of spirit, of joints and of marrow, and discerning the thoughts and intentions of the heart (Hebrews 4:12).

Jesus demonstrated the Word's effectiveness while being tempted by Satan. After He was assaulted by the devil's use of Scripture, He relied on His knowledge of the Word to combat the enemy. As a result, He was able to outsmart the devil at his own game. In our own lives, it is imperative we grow in our study of God's Word. We equip ourselves with wisdom and outsmart the enemy's attacks when we absorb Scripture.

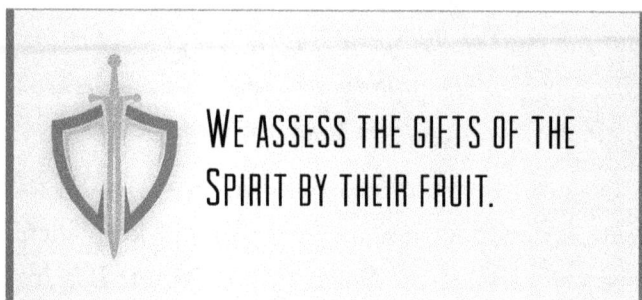

> # WE ASSESS THE GIFTS OF THE SPIRIT BY THEIR FRUIT.

During Jehoshaphat's reign, discovery and implementation of God's Word led to an entire nation's survival:

> *In the third year of his* [Jehoshaphat's] *reign he sent his officials...to teach in the cities of Judah.... And they taught in Judah, having the Book of the Law of the Lord with them. They went about through all the cities of Judah and taught among the people. And the fear of the Lord fell upon all the kingdoms of the lands that were around Judah, and they made no war against Jehoshaphat* (2 Chronicles 17:7, 9-10).

The passage further states how the Philistines, sworn enemies of Judah, brought gifts of tribute. When Judah studied God's Word, the fear of the Lord fell upon their enemies. This led to an era of peace. Jehoshaphat ushered in an era of peace and attained a nationwide shifting of atmospheres when he ingrained his kingdom's culture with the virtues of Scripture.

Joy, peace, and hope are other powerful spiritual weapons. In our fight against darkness, fruits of the Spirit like joy can carry us past the enemy's attacks. The Bible states:

> *Then he said to them, "Go your way. Eat the fat and drink sweet wine and send portions to anyone who has nothing ready, for this day is holy to our Lord. And do not be grieved, for the joy of the Lord is your strength"* (Nehemiah 8:10).

According to the Bible, we cannot possess strength apart from God's joy. It makes us capable of surviving even the bleakest seasons. Paul states:

> *Therefore, since we are surrounded by so great a cloud of witnesses, let us also lay aside every weight, and sin which clings so closely, and let us run with endurance the race that is set before us, looking to Jesus, the founder and perfecter of our faith, who for the joy that was set before him endured the cross, despising the shame, and is seated at the right hand of the throne of God* (Hebrews 12:1-2).

Even in something as terrible as the cross, Jesus saw the redemption of His orphaned brothers and sisters and pressed forward. Christ used joy to fuel His own perseverance in the midst of struggle.

Think about this the next time you face a severe hardship. Winston Churchill said, "If you're going through hell, keep going." The point is to keep our focus on the victory ahead and not get bogged down in present circumstances. By focusing on the reward, we push through and fix our eyes on God's unshakeable promises. King David wrote:

Even though I walk through the valley of the shadow of death, I will fear no evil, for you are with me (Psalm 23:4).

With joy and perseverance, our focus stays on the victory ahead and propels us forward.

Peace is another weapon of God's Kingdom that does not always make sense to our human minds. As Bill Johnson always says, "Peace is not the absence of conflict but the presence of security in God." Supernatural peace is God's perspective on things. God is an omniscient Being and therefore all-knowing. Nothing that happens surprises Him. Consequently, He is never worried. He becomes our peace because He is peace.

> BY FOCUSING ON THE REWARD, WE PUSH THROUGH AND FIX OUR EYES ON GOD'S UNSHAKEABLE PROMISES.

When peace becomes our default, we view things from a place of victory. From this vantage point, we discern attacks, hear God's strategies, and embrace a powerful stance.

How does peace become our default spiritual state? In the New Testament, the apostle John gives us a clue:

Peace I leave with you; my peace I give to you. Not as the world gives do I give to you. Let not your hearts be troubled, neither let them be afraid (John 14:27).

The Greek word for peace, *eirene* (eye-ray-nay), means a state of rest, quietness and calmness, an absence of strife; tranquility.[5]

As Bill Johnson reveals, Jesus is not talking about the peace experienced when there is no war but rather the state of remaining unshakable even in the midst of turmoil. This type of peace is supernatural. We do not work to attain it. It is already accomplished for us and comes as a gift from Jesus. The "peace I leave you" and the peace "I give to you" is actually His peace He gives to us.

The peace Jesus leaves for us is a fruit abiding in Him. As we connect to this fruit, we are grafted into Him as a branch is connected to the vine:

Do not be anxious about anything, but in everything by prayer and supplication with thanksgiving let your requests be made known to God. And the peace of God, which surpasses all understanding, will guard your hearts and your minds in Christ Jesus (Philippians 4:6-7).

As we embrace this gift, things that normally upset us bounce harmlessly off our shields. We become immune to the devil's fiery arrows as the Holy Spirit covers us with protection.

Jesus tells us, "Let not your heart be troubled, neither let it be afraid." Christ reminds us that we are responsible for stewarding our hearts and our peace. We are in charge of how we look at and react to each situation. This is important to remember when engaged in spiritual warfare. Oftentimes situations look bad, even hopeless. However, holding on to the truth of God's perspective calms even the darkest storms.

I remember walking around my neighborhood one day angry and frustrated about how things were going. I felt victimized by the trials our family faced. I put my earphones in my ears and listened to some music to distract myself, and instead of the expected music I heard Bill Johnson's voice say, "You know, every trial is a practice at a win!"

Whoa, I thought, *I'm not practicing my win.* In truth, I was practicing my skills of whining. This thought shifted my inner frustration to peace. I returned home eager to give up complaining and to begin my process of winning.

Hope, the confident expectation of good, is yet another tool we can wield in spiritual warfare. One of our congregants routinely reminds us that, "The person who has the most hope in the room has the most influence." Hope leaves the door open for God to fight for us in our circumstances. Without hope, our faith diminishes. Hope brings boldness and confidence in God. As we wield this weapon, it allows us to pray with faith and receive God's grace even after we make a mess.

Hope empowers us to believe and pray into the deliverance of impossible situations. To see breakthrough in our lives, we need to embrace hope:

And you will feel secure, because there is hope; you will look around and take your rest in security. You will lie down, and none will make you afraid; many will court your favor (Job 11:18-19).

The word *hope* in this passage translates as "things hoped for, expectation." When we carry an expectation for good (and especially when we see it fulfilled), that energy drives us into success. Solomon described this in one of his most famous proverbs:

Hope deferred makes the heart sick, but a desire fulfilled is a tree of life (Proverbs 13:12).

To navigate trials successfully, hope is critical. If you find yourself in a season without hope, turn your gaze to heaven and ask for a fresh release:

Rejoice in hope, be patient in tribulation, be constant in prayer (Romans 12:12).

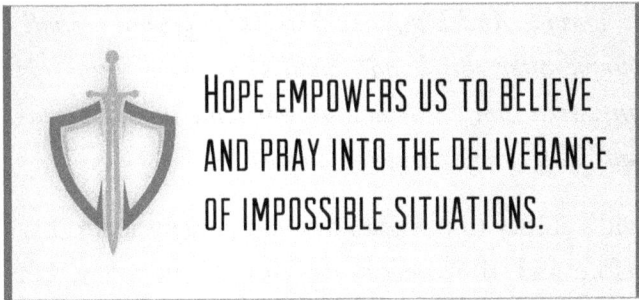

> HOPE EMPOWERS US TO BELIEVE AND PRAY INTO THE DELIVERANCE OF IMPOSSIBLE SITUATIONS.

The final spiritual weapon to be covered in this chapter is the ability to encourage one's self in the Lord. David was an expert at this both before and after becoming king. The Psalms are filled with passages where he, filled with doubt, brought his needs before the Father and allowed truth to change his perspective. Even in the darkest of passages, David managed to align himself with God's perspective:

> *The arrogant have hidden a trap for me, and with cords they have spread a net; beside the way they have set snares for me. Selah. I say to the Lord, You are my God; give ear to the voice of my pleas for mercy, O Lord! O Lord, my Lord, the strength of my salvation, you have covered my head in the day of battle* (Psalm 140:5-7).

> *And David was greatly distressed, for the people spoke of stoning him, because all the people were bitter in soul, each for his sons and daughters. But David strengthened himself in the Lord his God. And David said to Abiathar the priest, the son of Ahimelech, "Bring me the ephod." So Abiathar brought the ephod to David. And David inquired of the Lord, "Shall I pursue after this band? Shall I overtake them?" He answered him, "Pursue, for you shall surely overtake and shall surely rescue"* (1 Samuel 30:6-8).

David's ability to navigate discouragement led to his success both before and after becoming king. Even today, Christians admire his ferocity and dependence on God. Though his life was marked by sin, his repentant attitude earned him such a place in God's heart that he became part of the physical bloodline of Jesus.

Much of David's strength was his ability to stay focused on God's true nature—His goodness. This allowed him to engage in raw discussions with the Lord and to seize His destiny's promises. As we focus on God's goodness, we, too, can move deeper into our spiritual callings and rid ourselves of the filth of discouragement. Bill Johnson's book, *Strengthen Yourself in the Lord*, is an excellent tool for learning how to turn to God in the midst of crisis and remain encouraged.

NOTES

1. Stephen De Silva, "Hope Is a Handshake," Bethel.TV, August 19, 2015. http://www.bethel.tv/watch/3673/culture-of-hope/2015/09/16?session=1229.

2. "Shirtless in MY Offering," https://shop.bethel.com/collections/prosperous-soul/products/shirtless-in-my-offering.

3. "Praying it Forward," https://shop.bethel.com/collections/prosperous-soul/products/praying-it-forward.

4. "Praying from Power," https://shop.bethel.com/collections/dawna-de-silva/products/praying-from-power.

5. Blue Letter Bible, s.v. "Eirēnē," accessed February 14, 2017, https://www.blueletterbible.org/lang/lexicon/lexicon.cfm?Strongs=G1515&t=ESV.

CHAPTER FIVE

SPIRITUAL AUTHORITY

Several years back, I spoke at a conference where a sickly woman shared an unfortunate experience. While walking through her neighborhood, she noticed something odd about a house on her street. She believed it was haunted and, out of good intentions, decided to cast out any unclean spirits. Standing in front of the house, she declared, "Come out in Jesus's name!"

The demons did come out. Unfortunately, her spiritual authority was a few sizes too small. The demons attacked, and she spent the next two weeks battling an intense cough. When she asked why the evil spirits had been allowed to attack her, I replied, "Did you ask permission from the Holy Spirit before confronting them?" Her stunned silence that followed confirmed my suspicions.

What happened to this woman reminds me of the sons of Sceva in the Bible. In both cases, neither group carried sufficient spiritual authority. In the Sceva case, a group of untrained (and perhaps unsaved) Jews took it upon themselves to cast out demons in the name of Jesus. The problem was they had little to no relationship with God. When they entered the demon-possessed man's house, the evil spirit recognized their lack of authority and overpowered them. Sceva's sons ended up fleeing the house naked and bleeding:

> *Then some of the itinerant Jewish exorcists undertook to invoke the name of the Lord Jesus over those who had evil spirits, saying, "I adjure you by the Jesus whom Paul proclaims." Seven sons of a Jewish high priest named Sceva were doing this. But the evil spirit answered them, "Jesus I know, and Paul I recognize, but who are you?" And the man in whom was the evil spirit leaped on them, mastered all of them and overpowered them, so that they fled out of that house naked and wounded* (Acts 19:13-16).

I believe that when we operate outside of God's will, we face the possibility of stepping outside of His protection. A good friend of mine, Cyndi Barber, likens it to walking out from under an umbrella while standing in the rain. Just as it would be foolish to leave an umbrella's covering in the midst of a storm, it would be impossible to leave the Lord's covering and not be affected.

I believe this is one of the reasons Jesus only did what He saw His Father doing. Discerning God's hand of protection,

Jesus stayed within the reins of His assignment and only stepped out when He felt certain prompts coincided with the Father's will:

And behold, a Canaanite woman from that region came out and was crying, "Have mercy on me, O Lord, Son of David; my daughter is severely oppressed by a demon." But he did not answer her a word. And his disciples came and begged him, saying, "Send her away, for she is crying out after us." He answered, "I was sent only to the lost sheep of the house of Israel." But she came and knelt before him, saying, "Lord, help me." And he answered, "It is not right to take the children's bread and throw it to the dogs." She said, "Yes, Lord, yet even the dogs eat the crumbs that fall from their masters' table." Then Jesus answered her, "O woman, great is your faith! Be it done for you as you desire." And her daughter was healed instantly (Matthew 15:22-28).

> JUST AS IT WOULD BE FOOLISH TO LEAVE AN UMBRELLA'S COVERING IN THE MIDST OF A STORM, IT WOULD BE IMPOSSIBLE TO LEAVE THE LORD'S COVERING AND NOT BE AFFECTED.

Paul discussed the Lord's covering while writing of his extensive ministry trip:

And they went through the region of Phrygia and Galatia, having been forbidden by the Holy Spirit to speak the word in Asia (Acts 16:6).

I wonder what might have happened had Paul refused to obey the Holy Spirit. This may have left him vulnerable to a spiritual attack or slowed the effectiveness of his ministry. Though I do not believe God abandons His followers, I wonder how often our spiritual authority is weakened through acts of disobedience. Though all authority in heaven and on earth has been given to Christ, we—His ambassadors—have boundaries assigned to us by God that we must honor.

Understanding our spiritual boundaries will give us security. It will also encourage us to steward our connection with the Father. Without relying on His presence, we may find ourselves entering into unguarded territory. Take the story of Jesus and the Canaanite woman, for example. Had the Father explicitly told Jesus not to intervene, Christ simply would have ignored the woman and passed on. We can assume this because Jesus only did what He saw the Father doing (see John 5:19). But when He sensed the Father's heart being moved by this woman's faith, Jesus stepped outside of His original assignment (deliverance for the Jews) and extended a gift of miraculous intervention. If Jesus only did what He saw His Father doing, how much more should we adhere to His example?

Jesus is our model, so we too need to steward a strong connection with the Father. As we engage in our individual, God-given destinies, we need to be aware of the Spirit's promptings. This enables us to act in situations where we may not normally feel called to intervene. This is the powerful Christian's life. As we co-labor with Him to see heaven's

Kingdom invade earth, our hearts listen to the commands of heaven so we can adjust our paths accordingly.

The apostle Paul is another hero in the Lord's army who exemplified reliance on the Holy Spirit. When God's Spirit told him not to go to Asia, he obeyed. When the Lord prompted him to visit Jerusalem (even against his followers' wishes), he listened.

Just because someone uses the name *Jesus* does not mean they are under proper spiritual authority. Such was shown with the sons of Sceva. Though God can bless a person's good intentions, it is His will that we ultimately co-labor with Him. This reliance on His presence, cultivated daily, is what brings about success in the Kingdom.

Francis Frangipane, author of *The Three Battlegrounds*, asserts that spiritual authority (as exemplified through Jesus), is obtained through humility and acts of surrender. Scripture says:

> *But he gives more grace. Therefore it says, "God opposes the proud but gives grace to the humble"* (James 4:6).

This may seem foreign to us in our human societies where success is often attributed to talent and ambition. In God's Kingdom, however, people advance according to how much they are willing to sacrifice. Jesus gave the greatest sacrifice of all—His life. This is why He was given the ultimate promotion:

> *Therefore God has highly exalted him and bestowed on him the name that is above every name, so that at the name of Jesus every knee should bow, in heaven and on earth and under the earth, and every tongue*

confess that Jesus Christ is Lord, to the glory of God the Father (Philippians 2:9-11).

Because of Christ's willingness to sacrifice, God exalted Him above everything else.

We too are called to live a life of sacrifice. Yet, this does not mean we must all unhealthily sacrifice in hopes of attaining greatness. We should never approach the Father with formulas in hopes of a specific result. That is manipulation. True humility and surrender comes as an act of love. Once we grasp this concept, we surrender ourselves willingly and live our lives according to our individual purposes.

If you desire to grow in spiritual authority, you must give up everything for God and this must come as an act of love. Jesus said:

> *If anyone comes to me and does not hate his own father and mother and wife and children and brothers and sisters, yes, and even his own life, he cannot be my disciple. Whoever does not bear his own cross and come after me cannot be my disciple. For which of you, desiring to build a tower, does not first sit down and count the cost, whether he has enough to complete it?* (Luke 14:26-28)

Following Jesus will cost you everything. Although the gift of salvation is free, being a true follower of Jesus requires every ounce of your being.

As we grow in spiritual authority, our mission to transmit God's Kingdom to the earth increases in capacity. In Matthew, Jesus was given *all* authority and commissioned us to retake dominion over the planet (see Matt. 28:18; Luke 10:19). Though we have authority and dominion in Christ, God is still a respecter of boundaries. This is why certain unclean spirits have authority over persons, cities, and regions.

People who partner with evil spirits through sin, ignorance, or lies hand over the "keys" to their spiritual domains. This gives the enemy legal access to their lives and opens doors for demonic harassment. If this is the case, the unclean spirits may not be easily removed until the partnerships are renounced.

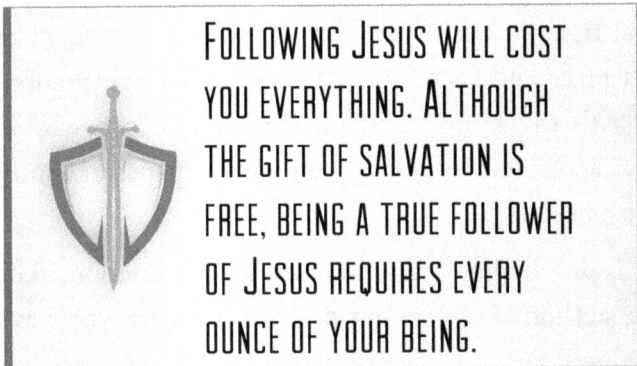

> FOLLOWING JESUS WILL COST YOU EVERYTHING. ALTHOUGH THE GIFT OF SALVATION IS FREE, BEING A TRUE FOLLOWER OF JESUS REQUIRES EVERY OUNCE OF YOUR BEING.

If you find yourself praying for individuals who suffer from a demonic spirit, work with them to see if this demon exists because of legal access. If so, pray with them to release God's forgiveness and ask what the Lord wishes to impart in its place. If they do not want to sever ties with the demonic, then it may be wise to not try to deliver them at all. Jesus gave the warning in Matthew:

Now when the unclean spirit goes out of a man, it passes through waterless places seeking rest, and does not find it. Then it says, "I will return to my house from which I came"; and when it comes, it finds it unoccupied, swept, and put in order. Then it goes and takes along with it seven other spirits more wicked than itself, and they go in and live there; and the last state of that man becomes worse than the first. That is the way it will also be with this evil generation (Matthew 12:43-45 NASB).

I have found this to be of great significance when shifting atmospheres. Just because a demon exists in a person or location does not mean it is always wise to simply cast it out. Find the legal right or open door that allows the demon to exist in the first place and then begin the process of deliverance. Partnering with the Holy Spirit to gain insight into why a spirit exists in a certain area or region can help permanently shift an atmosphere.

Sin is an obvious reason for demonic habitation. Although we have authority to cast out demons, persons who have been delivered will fail to successfully defend their newly found freedom if they do not fill the newly vacated areas with Christ. People can gain lasting authority over the devil if they break ties and tear up the "root" issues that existed in their lives.

Another stronghold for the enemy is unbelief. Jesus faced this in His hometown of Nazareth. Encountering unbelief, the Messiah Himself experienced a limitation to His power:

And Jesus said to them, "A prophet is not without honor, except in his hometown and among his relatives and in his own household." And he could do no mighty work there, except that he laid his hands on a few sick people and healed them. And he marveled because of their unbelief. And he went about among the villages teaching (Mark 6:4-6).

Faith is paramount for wielding spiritual authority. Matthew writes:

When they came to the crowd, a man came up to Jesus, falling on his knees before Him and saying, "Lord, have mercy on my son, for he is a lunatic and is very ill; for he often falls into the fire and often into the water. I brought him to Your disciples, and they could not cure him." And Jesus answered and said, "You unbelieving and perverted generation, how long shall I be with you? How long shall I put up with you? Bring him here to Me." And Jesus rebuked him, and the demon came out of him, and the boy was cured at once. Then the disciples came to Jesus privately and said, "Why could we not drive it out?" And He said to them, "Because of the littleness of your faith; for truly I say to you, if you have faith the size of a mustard seed, you will say to this mountain, 'Move from here to there,' and it will move; and nothing will be impossible to you" (Matthew 17:14-20 NASB).

When we partner with unbelief, we forfeit our God-given right to co-labor with Christ. In contrast, when we cultivate faith, we increase our authority by placing full confidence in God.

If we want to grow in spiritual authority, we must be willing to lay down our lives for the purposes of God. Total acts of surrender lead to trust, which activates faith, which in turn results in God increasing our authority.

Jesus's parables continually rewarded those who proved themselves to be trustworthy. In the parable of the talents, God took from the servant who failed to steward anything and gave it to the one who stewarded the most. God is in the business of stewardship. Once He hands us an assignment, it is our responsibility to complete it. If you need inspiration for this, look to Jesus. He had the greatest assignment of all and passed it with flying colors.

> WHEN WE CULTIVATE FAITH, WE INCREASE OUR AUTHORITY BY PLACING FULL CONFIDENCE IN GOD.

In our quest for growing spiritual authority, we must never underestimate the power of collective prayer. Not only does it raise our level of faith, but it also creates an opening for Jesus to attend our meetings. Jesus told His disciples:

Truly, I say to you, whatever you bind on earth shall be bound in heaven, and whatever you loose on earth shall be loosed in heaven. Again I say to you, if two of you agree on earth about anything they ask, it will be done for them by my Father in heaven. For where two or three are gathered in my name, there am I among them (Matthew 18:18-20).

If Jesus is in the midst of our groups, it is no wonder the enemy tries to separate us through offense, bitterness, and fear. When shifting atmospheres over regions, I make sure to operate in a group setting so we are all in one accord.

When shifting atmospheres, do not forget the power of the angelic realm. Some of these supernatural beings are there to help you. Ask God to release His angels over your situations and watch as you gain the upper hand in the battle against darkness. Just as God dispatched Michael to release the messenger for Daniel's breakthrough, so too the soldiers of God wait to fight on our behalf.

CHAPTER SIX

SPIRITUAL ATMOSPHERES

And you were dead in the trespasses and sins in which you once walked, following the course of this world, following the prince of the power of the air, the spirit that is now at work in the sons of disobedience…But God, being rich in mercy, because of the great love with which he loved us, even when we were dead in our trespasses, made us alive together with Christ—by grace you have been saved—and raised us up with him and seated us with him in the heavenly places in Christ Jesus.

—Ephesians 2:1-2, 4-6

We can define the word *atmosphere* as a pervading tone or mood. *Spiritual* is something invisible as opposed to a material or physical entity. When I talk about spiritual atmospheres, I am referring to the invisible (spiritual) tones or moods hovering over an individual, community, city, or region.

Some people believe that ungodly atmospheres are the same thing as demonic spirits. While I do believe demonic atmospheres are presided over by the demonic realm, I do not believe the atmospheres themselves are actual demons. Atmospheres, for me, are the prevailing spiritual realities created by man's partnership with the entities residing in the spiritual realm. As the messages these spiritual beings emit are agreed upon and partnered with, the resulting atmosphere expands. Therefore, I see atmospheres, both godly and ungodly, as cyclical partnerings between broadcasts from the spirit realm and man's participation with them.

Many of us have experienced spiritually "thin" places or open heavens. These are areas where the accumulation of worship and prayer has released the tangible presence of God. In these places, healings, salvations, signs, and wonders are more easily attained than in more spiritually "thick" areas. These thick places are environments where negative spiritual climates have been allowed to develop. In areas governed by a religious spirit, for instance, the prophetic tends to not flow as freely.

I see the development of negative atmospheres as a result of people partnering with sin, lies, or the demonic. As humans partner with these things, more and more evil spirits are attracted. This results in the development of a negative spiritual climate from which demonic forces can operate.

For example, if a married couple allow sin into their lives by viewing pornography, an open door is created in which the demonic is actually invited into their home. These demons, now given a legal right to harass and torment, gladly take up residence and work to sow further seeds of discord in their marriage. If this harassment is not dealt with through repentance and closing the door to pornography, then a negative spiritual climate will develop.

The more people agree with these evil spirits and their messages through partnerships with sin, the more powerful the atmospheres become. This is how strongholds develop. Strongholds, areas of particular resistance, grow as people partner with lies, sin, and demonic broadcasts. Whether these broadcasts are transmissions of *fear, hate, perversion,* or *self-loathing,* they weaken a person's spiritual and emotional health and cause havoc.

When evil spirits gain a place of power over a region, they broadcast lies over the entire area—much like a radio station. We have the capacity to either "tune in" to these channels or to switch them off. Part of our responsibility in tuning out the enemy's voice is for us to switch the channel we are listening to that is emitting a sinful broadcast, but doing so does not actually shut off its transmissions into the airwaves. We need to release God's opposing messages into the airwaves to actually stop these transmissions.

<hr />

Let's use Hollywood as an example of atmospheres. Hollywood gets a lot of criticism from the church, and rightfully so; it is a definite stronghold of perversion and entitlement, and its agendas are spewed throughout the world in the guise of entertainment. Although I fully endorse boycotting movies and companies whose agendas do not align with God's Word, boycotting by itself is not enough to shift Hollywood's atmosphere. We must also replace the broadcast being produced and released by funding entertainment that releases godly virtues.

If I do not release God's opposite, I am simply exercising my skill in ignoring the enemy's voice. To displace a negative atmosphere, we must release one of our own. This is why my husband and I have consistently supported Christian radio for over thirty years. We are purposely helping to release an opposing voice into the airwaves.

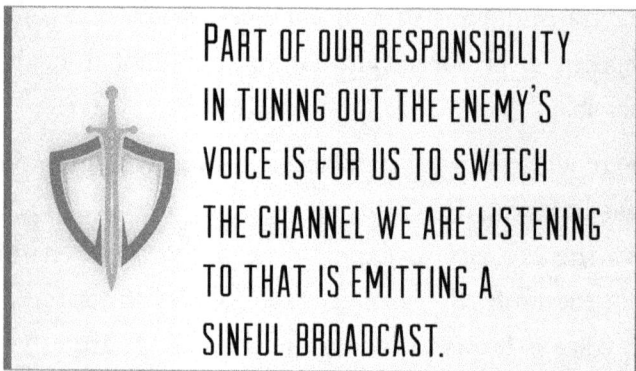

> PART OF OUR RESPONSIBILITY IN TUNING OUT THE ENEMY'S VOICE IS FOR US TO SWITCH THE CHANNEL WE ARE LISTENING TO THAT IS EMITTING A SINFUL BROADCAST.

If we want to take back our cities and install heavenly atmospheres over them, we must learn how to discern the enemy's broadcasts. Once we do this, we can renounce their effects and replace them with God's truth. We will cover discerning atmospheres in more detail in Chapter Seven.

When we discern a thought, feeling, or mood coming from an atmosphere, we can best defend against them through *displacement*. Displacement follows a pattern of renouncement and replacement (which we will go into later) that actually replaces the ungodly atmosphere with a godly one.

My favorite phrase for rejecting broadcasts is, "I *see* you and I am not partnering with you. I send you back in Jesus's name." I then wait on the Holy Spirit to direct me as how to counteract the atmosphere. Sometimes, He has me release the opposite; other times, He has me release something totally different. We will discuss this more in future chapters. Consider this a teaser to whet your appetite.

As we mentioned earlier, spiritual atmospheres do not have to be negative; they can also be positive and align with God's Kingdom. These ecosystems send out messages of their own. I call them heavenly broadcasts or "virtues," as Bill Johnson calls them. These are the heavenly promises or truths swirling around in these heavenly environments. In my husband's manual, *Prosperous Soul Foundations*, Bill Johnson's quotes are used to explore this topic:

> Heaven also has broadcasts we can tune into. These are called *virtues*…These sound like, "God is in a good mood," "There is more than enough," or "I can do all things in Christ!" Virtues…need to be tuned in to, and this tuning is one of the activities of displacement. Other activities include intercession, worship, and declaration. This is why it is so

effective to play worship music or read scripture when you are [engaging in spiritual warfare].[1]

These virtues, grounded in Scripture, have the power to save, heal, and resurrect. When imparted over a person, place, or region, they displace demonic spirits, atmospheres, and strongholds. Paul encourages this indwelling of truth in his letter to the Philippians:

> *Finally, brothers, whatever is true, whatever is honorable, whatever is just, whatever is pure, whatever is lovely, whatever is commendable, if there is any excellence, if there is anything worthy of praise, think about these things* (Philippians 4:8).

When we partner with and act according to God's truths, the enemy's lies and demonic broadcasts shatter. As we trust in God, we weaken the enemy's hold over our lives and spiritual territories (homes, cities, regions). Obedience becomes an act of warfare:

> *And if you faithfully obey the voice of the Lord your God, being careful to do all his commandments…the Lord your God will set you high above all the nations of the earth. …Blessed shall you be in the city, and blessed shall you be in the field. Blessed shall be the fruit of your womb and the fruit of your ground and the fruit of your cattle, the increase of your herds and the young of your flock* (Deuteronomy 28:1,3-4).

Bill Johnson states that "Whenever a demonic spirit rules over a city, the church is either in direct conflict with its presence or partnering with it."[2] If negative spiritual climates inhabit a city, it is the church's responsibility to react by releasing God's opposing truth. The saints' next mission is to steward these truths and steep their community in the promises of God. Just as cities can be afflicted with mindsets of hate, wickedness, or violence, so can entire regions be filled with love, purity, and peace.

The devil works hard to implement his agendas of hate, corruption, and separation. This is why certain cities house unusually high divorce, murder, and suicide rates. Bent on leading these areas into destruction, the devil works to ingrain his agendas into the minds of the people encased within the environments.

The church wins this battle by collaborating with God's work and by releasing His virtues into the community. If a city is steeped in poverty, the church releases prosperity. If an area is riddled with crime, the church partners with God to release safety and justice.

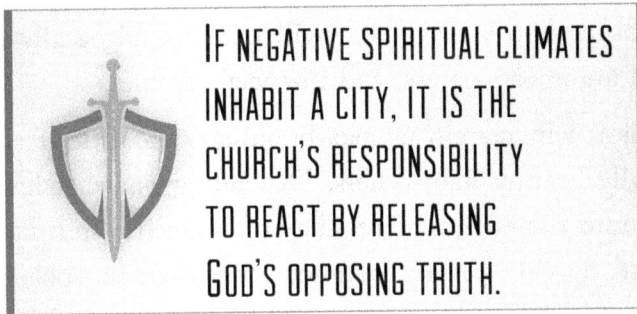

> **IF NEGATIVE SPIRITUAL CLIMATES INHABIT A CITY, IT IS THE CHURCH'S RESPONSIBILITY TO REACT BY RELEASING GOD'S OPPOSING TRUTH.**

As servants of Christ, our job is to come up against ungodly atmospheres and replace them with heavenly ones. We do this by supplanting Satan's broadcasts (sinful messages) with those of heaven. Whatever we discern the enemy's broadcast to be, we reverse it through an invitation of God's truth. God's ways are always more powerful. Once we release God's truth through prayer into the atmosphere, the enemy's influence has to bow. Changing atmospheres in regions is accomplished not only in prayer gatherings but also by infusing our communities with godly oversight, teachings, and community outreach.

Another way to view spiritual atmospheres is as Kris Vallotton does in his book, *Heavy Rain*—as ecosystems or environments.[3] *Ecosystems* are the biological communities formed by interacting organisms and their physical environment. Ecosystems are created with ingredients the biological organisms seed into that environment, and is why rainforests, deserts, and oceans have ecosystems specific to their biological makeup.

The same is true of humans and their spiritual environments. If a husband and wife fill their marriage with rage and intimidation, an ecosystem (or atmosphere) of fear will develop. Left unsolved, this ecosystem will manifest physically in the form of arguments, stress, and financial troubles.

This is why certain people, buildings, and cities feel more spiritually healthy than others. Depending on what has been seeded into the environment, the area's specific spiritual realities will develop. Jesus illustrated this when he spoke about how good trees bear good fruit and bad trees bear bad fruit (see Matt. 7:17-18). Whatever we sow into our environments eventually takes root—whether it be peace or strife, love or hate.

This is how families, cities, and regions become stuck in cycles of poverty, fear, and powerlessness. Failing to steward their spiritual environments, people open doors to the demonic. Unless we are able to identify the root issues and replace them with the Lord's truth, we will not be able to break free and experience freedom.

* * *

Another way to understand atmospheres and how they shift in our lives is to look at our relationships with movies. I remember as a teenager sneaking into films like *Jaws* and *Friday the Thirteenth*. I taunted my friends with phrases like *I'm not scared* and *I'm braver than you* making the movie-going experience somewhat a competition. We would see who could stay in their seats the longest and avoid succumbing to the terror. Unfortunately, I never made it long enough to collect any prizes.

Like atmospheres, films naturally affect/shift the hearts and minds of the audience. When we enter a theater, our thoughts, feelings, and moods change as we undergo the process of entertainment. As the story unfolds, our willing suspension of disbelief (our agreement with the story as reality to better engage with its emotions) kicks in. We experience the tonal shifts of the film and adjust our empathy accordingly.

When we watch films like *Raiders of the Lost Ark,* our personal atmospheres shift from excitement to thrills and adventure. If it is a romantic tragedy like *Titanic,* our atmospheres morph from hope to sadness. Each of these shifts is predetermined by the author who structured the story. As long as we continue to "buy into" these created realities, our hearts and minds will follow the movie's currents.

This process is no different from how we buy into and cooperate with spiritual atmospheres. When we "buy into" their broadcasts, whether good or bad, we give them authority over us. For instance, if we walk into a store feeling depressed but suddenly encounter a sense or feeling that *God is good*, we can either agree with that statement and live under its influence or shrug it off and lose its heavenly impact. Hopefully, we will partner with our willful suspension of disbelief (our acceptance of something as reality) and accept that virtue as reality. We can then walk through the rest of our day believing that God is good and stewarding this truth into our lives.

This is why you can leave your house in the best of moods only to have it fluctuate into a range of emotions. Let's say you leave your house joyful; yet, when you arrive at the grocery store, you experience anxiety. Moments before you were in the best of moods yet now you are doused in stress and anxiety. What happened? Chances are you "picked up" an ungodly atmosphere's message and started partnering with it and took it on as your own.

As we learn to identify the atmospheres and broadcasts pervading our area, we grow in understanding how to defend or adopt them as truth. In this following example, a former client, Julie, discovered the power of rejecting negative atmospheres and renouncing their broadcasts.

> THE CHURCH IS DESIGNED TO OPERATE AS BRINGERS OF THE KINGDOM OF GOD AND TO RELEASE HOPE, PEACE, AND PROSPERITY INTO THESE COMMUNITIES WHERE DEMONS WORK TO RELEASE THE OPPOSITE.

Julie always slept well—some would say like a rock. When she dreamed, her dreams were usually encouraging and fun. But around the age of forty, she started having nightmares. These night visions were so vivid and demonic that they forced her to cry out in her sleep. Sometimes, her cries were so loud that they woke her husband.

She found herself experiencing these repeated nightmares and constantly tried to wake herself up. During these encounters, demons weighed her down and tried to keep her from waking. These dreams terrified her so much that she began fearing sleep itself. This fear eventually crept into her day. Consequently, she began to feel on edge nearly all day long.

The atmosphere in her home no longer felt safe; instead, it felt hostile and cruel. This went on for weeks. One day, she visited the nearby park for fresh air. While jogging, a stranger's dog broke loose from its leash and chased her. Julie screamed and ran so hard that she wet her pants. When the owners caught up to take hold of their dog, they were amazed. They had never seen their dog act like that before.

Julie returned home and wondered if it were possible the neighbor's dog had picked up her own partnering with fear. If so, she realized she was actually handing over power to the enemy. She called a friend who encouraged her to take authority over her home and dream life. Hanging up, Julie blasted worship music and recited Psalms all throughout the house. She anointed each doorway with oil and even went up to the attic to release peace. Following these acts, her fears shifted and the atmosphere over her mind and home changed. From that day on, the nightmares stopped.

Julie learned a valuable lesson. Partnering with this atmosphere of fear allowed its presence to increase in her life and even began to broadcast from her to her natural surroundings. As long as she continued to "buy into" its anxiety, the evil spirit was able to operate with power. When she finally took ownership and renounced its hold over her life, the atmosphere and its relating messages lifted.

Just as Julie's partnership with fear gave it increasing power, demonic strongholds grow as communities digress from God's Word and embrace lifestyles of sin. As more people partner with the messages that are announced, the demonic influence grows. This cycle continues until either repentance is made, truth is revealed, or God intervenes. The church is designed to operate as bringers of the Kingdom of God and to release hope, peace, and prosperity into these communities where demons work to release the opposite.

About a month before we were scheduled to do our very first Shifting Atmospheres conference, I received a phone call from an intercessor friend. She wanted us to seek the Lord in prayer regarding a demonic influence that was gaining traction among the youth in her county. Several young teens had committed suicide, and while she and some friends had been praying around the schools, news of suicide pacts had been exposed. Teen suicides swept so strongly through the community that even some of her church's family members bore the pain of personal loss.

Before we finished the conference, we gathered together all willing participants and placed them in four groups to signify north, south, east, and west. Guided by the Holy Spirit, I led them in a quick prayer of repentance. Because we were dealing with an assignment of death, the prayer went something like this:

> *I ask You, God, to forgive me if I have ever partnered with a spirit of helplessness, hopelessness, secrecy, murder, or death, and I forgive anyone in our community who has partnered with these spirits. We release hope, vision, and life back into our region, and we command this attack on our youth to stop immediately in Jesus's name.*

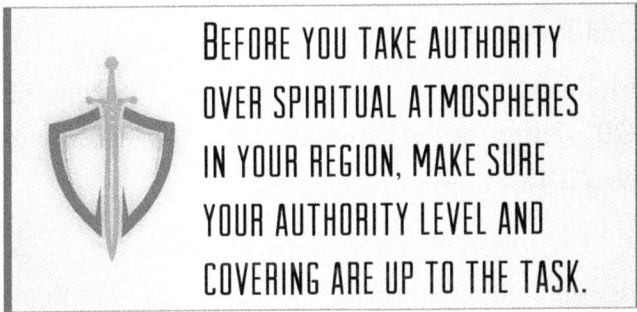

> BEFORE YOU TAKE AUTHORITY OVER SPIRITUAL ATMOSPHERES IN YOUR REGION, MAKE SURE YOUR AUTHORITY LEVEL AND COVERING ARE UP TO THE TASK.

One of our sons, Cory, had written a song, "Dissipate,"[4] a few years back that had an anointing to break suicide. I had him stand on stage and play it in the background while we prayed. We were encouraged to find out weeks later the teen suicide pacts had been exposed and the accompanying suicides stopped.

Before you take authority over spiritual atmospheres in your region, make sure your authority level and covering are up to the task. To begin, start stewarding your own internal atmospheres before branching out into the external ones around you. As you grow in your understanding of atmospheres and the authority you carry, begin practicing in your own home. As you steward your authority and the territory God has given you, more will be granted:

> *For to everyone who has will more be given, and he will have an abundance. But from the one who has not, even what he has will be taken away* (Matthew 25:29).

NOTES

1. Stephen De Silva, *Prosperous Soul Foundations* (Accent Digital Publishing, 2010).

2. Bill Johnson, "Born into a War," Bethel.TV, November 14, 2016, http://www.bethel.tv/watch/4497/born-into -a-war/2016/11/14.

3. Kris Vallotton, *Heavy Rain* (Regal, 2010), 988.

4. "Dissipate" from the album, *Someday When I'm Young,* (to purchase album) https://shop.bethel.com/products/ someday-when-i-m-young.

CHAPTER SEVEN

FINDING YOUR NORMAL

And he gave the apostles, the prophets, the
evangelists, the shepherds and teachers, to equip
the saints for the work of ministry, for building
up the body of Christ, until we all attain to the
unity of the faith and of the knowledge of the Son
of God, to mature manhood, to the measure of the
stature of the fullness of Christ, so that we may no
longer be children, tossed to and fro by the waves
and carried about by every wind of doctrine, by
human cunning, by craftiness in deceitful schemes.
—EPHESIANS 4:11-14

Our ability to discern atmospheres, spirits, and mindsets comes after we first establish our *normal*. By normal, I mean how we think and feel on a regular basis. Our normals are made up of the internal truths that govern our lives. These can be truths like *God is good* and *He loves me all the time* or lies (false truths) like *nobody wants me* or *I am unloved*.

Christians who have a healthy normal easily discern the enemy's atmospheres/lies because the voices feel foreign. For instance, if a person who is driving suddenly has a thought of veering into oncoming traffic, his understanding of what is "normal" (driving safely) keeps him from steering into the wrong lane.

Establishing your normal helps to decipher which thoughts are not your own. The enemy uses a myriad of voices (whisperings, taunts, impressions) to try and deceive you. Self-awareness empowers you to switch off these enemy channels and, instead, tune in to heaven's broadcasts instead.

The chart below helps to expose what healthy and unhealthy normals can look like. You may want to circle any mindsets that seem familiar:

HEALTHY NORMAL	UNHEALTHY NORMAL
COURAGE:	**FEAR:**
<ul><li>*I can do all things through Christ who strengthens me* (Phil. 4:13).</li><li>I am powerful in Christ (2 Tim. 1:7).</li><li>God is my protector (Ps. 91).</li></ul>	<ul><li>There is no way I can do this.</li><li>I am not smart enough to pull this off.</li><li>No one is for me. I have to protect myself.</li></ul>

HEALTHY NORMAL	UNHEALTHY NORMAL
ACCEPTED: - I am a child of God (Rom. 8:15). - My colleagues value me even when we disagree (Prov. 27:17).	**REJECTED:** - I feel like God does not even know I exist. - No one wants to hear my opinion.
PEACE: - Even in the hard times, God is with me (Phil. 4:7). - Even as I rest, God is protecting me (Rom. 16:20).	**STRESS:** - I just want it all to end. I cannot handle it. - What am I doing? This was such a bad idea.
LOVE: - I am so excited to share the love of God with others (Matt. 5:16). - I may not like you right now but I am going to respect you (James 1:19).	**SELFISHNESS:** - These people are a waste of my time. - I will invest into this relationship but only if I get something back.
SELF-CONTROL: - I choose to forgive my wife for not meeting my needs. - That looks fun but it is probably not the best decision (Matt. 5:29).	**PERVERSION:** - I'll just go take care of these needs myself. - I am so miserable so I will just do it anyway.
ACCEPTANCE: - *I am fearfully and wonderfully made* (Ps. 139:14).	**SELF-HATRED:** - I feel like I am a mistake.
PROSPERITY: - God wants to bless me (Phil. 4:19). - God knows what I need (Matt. 6:31).	**POVERTY:** - I just have to work harder for what I need. - I will never have enough.

HEALTHY NORMAL	UNHEALTHY NORMAL
PURPOSE: • God has plans for my life (Jer. 29:11). • God is going to make sure I get where I am supposed to be (Phil. 1:6).	**AIMLESSNESS:** • Why am I alive? • I am afraid of missing my call.
HOPE: • I can succeed at this (Rom. 5:5). • God will defend me (Ps. 62:2).	**HOPELESSNESS:** • What if I fail? • Why expect good things to happen?
JOY: • I can experience laughter throughout the day (Ps. 16:11). • Even though this is hard, I know God is working His plan through me (James 1:2).	**SADNESS:** • I am so lonely and unhappy. • Everyone is against me.

If you discover any unhealthy mindsets in your life, take some time to examine each one and ask the Holy Spirit where they first gained influence. This mindset will often stem from a childhood memory. In most Sozo sessions, people receive healing once they uncover a deep wound from childhood and exchange it for God's truth. Take some time right now for inner healing and ask the Holy Spirit these questions:

1. Holy Spirit, which ungodly mindset do I need to examine?

2. Holy Spirit, where did I first learn the lie that created this mindset?

3. Is there anyone I need to forgive?

4. I hand You this lie, Holy Spirit. What truth do You want to impart in its place?

5. Holy Spirit, would you remove all ungodly mindsets attached to this lie and any harm it has caused me or others?

6. Holy Spirit, what Scripture or verse do You want to show me to emphasize this new belief?

This process is a condensed version of an inquiry prayer we use in Sozo sessions. To learn more about this process, check out my previous book, *Sozo: Saved, Healed, Delivered*.

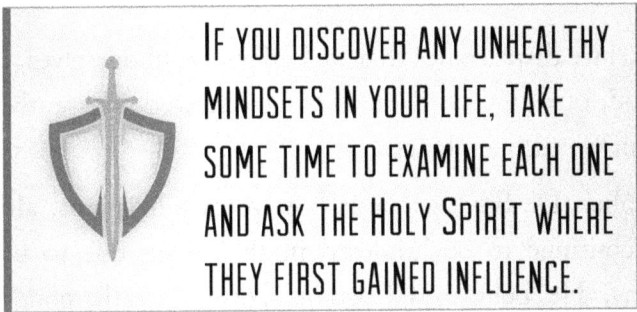

> IF YOU DISCOVER ANY UNHEALTHY MINDSETS IN YOUR LIFE, TAKE SOME TIME TO EXAMINE EACH ONE AND ASK THE HOLY SPIRIT WHERE THEY FIRST GAINED INFLUENCE.

You may wonder why we need to do this process of renewal. The Bible says we have the mind of Christ (see 1 Cor. 2:16). If so, why take the time to constantly cleanse our minds? The answer is that although we have the mind of Christ, we must continue to adhere to His principles.

To replace our ungodly beliefs, we must realize they do not line up with God's intention for our lives. It is impossible for any belief system based on a lie to produce good fruit. If we ask the Holy Spirit to reveal lies and supplant them with truth, we can develop a healthy normal.

God constantly encourages us to renew our minds:

> *We are destroying speculations and every lofty thing raised up against the knowledge of God, and we are taking every thought captive to the obedience of Christ* (2 Corinthians 10:5 NASB).

> *And do not be conformed to this world, but be transformed by the renewing of your mind, so that you may prove what the will of God is, that which is good and acceptable and perfect* (Romans 12:2 NASB).

Until we displace lies that we believe about ourselves, others, and God, our minds will need to be renewed constantly. Only then can we fully embrace truth.

Stephen De Silva explains how most Christians, although saved, continue to be hindered in their lives due to ungodly mindsets. He believes Christians become really good "fruit pickers" and pick the bad fruit from their lives rather than conform themselves to Christ's image. Instead of trying to cover up our messes, we can make our trees (hearts) good by uprooting the issues the Holy Spirit exposes in our lives.

> *Either make the tree good and its fruit good, or make the tree bad and its fruit bad; for the tree is known by its fruit. You brood of vipers, how can you, being evil, speak what is good? For the mouth speaks out of that which fills the heart* (Matthew 12:33-34 NASB).

> *Likewise, every good tree bears good fruit, but a bad tree bears bad fruit. A good tree cannot bear bad fruit,*

and a bad tree cannot bear good fruit. Every tree that does not bear good fruit is cut down and thrown into the fire (Matthew 7:17-19 NIV).

Instead of hiding our bad fruit, we should uproot the bad trees and replace them with good ones. Making the trees good, Steve says, comes from tearing out the roots in our lives that represent bad trees. These bad trees are nothing more than false mindsets/lies. We must uproot them to seize God's truth.

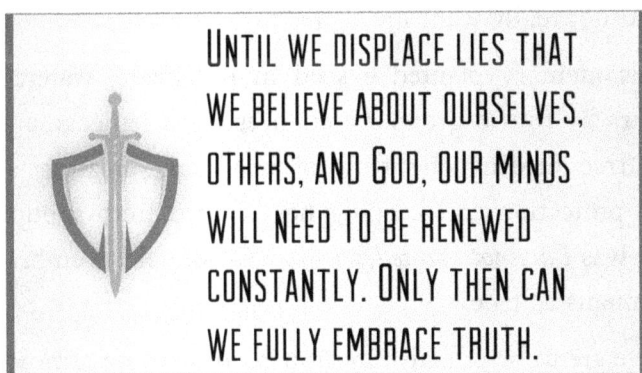

> ## UNTIL WE DISPLACE LIES THAT WE BELIEVE ABOUT OURSELVES, OTHERS, AND GOD, OUR MINDS WILL NEED TO BE RENEWED CONSTANTLY. ONLY THEN CAN WE FULLY EMBRACE TRUTH.

Years ago, a friend came in for her session. She had already experienced breakthrough many times before. When asked why she wanted to schedule another, she stated that she simply felt "unwanted" whenever she was invited to social gatherings. No matter how many people told her, "I'm so glad you are here," she always felt unwanted.

We asked the Holy Spirit to show her where she first learned this lie. The Lord showed her a memory from a time she was almost three years old. In the memory, she stood outside her home and heard roaring laughter inside. Curious, she opened the front door and stepped inside. When she did, the people in the living room looked her way and instantly stopped laughing. The Holy Spirit told her, "You believed the lie that they did not want you in the room."

When we asked Jesus for the truth, she started to laugh. She said Jesus told her they stopped laughing because they were planning her surprise birthday party for the next day. I asked her if she remembered the birthday party. She said, "Yes. I walked into the room and everyone yelled 'surprise,' but I felt they did not really want me there."

This memory planted a seed in her heart, watered over the years by future group experiences until it became a fully grown tree bearing the fruit of rejection—creating a need for self-protection and keeping her isolated from groups. Her normal was *I am not wanted*, so she was not able to embrace any compliments as true.

If we are to be effective in properly discerning atmospheres, we must make each and every tree (mindset) in our lives good.

Once we have established a new healthy normal, we can discern which thoughts are our own and which thoughts are the enemy's. Once we identify our normal thoughts, we can decipher enemy broadcasts—those echoes in our brains that originate from the demonic realm. When we realize these thoughts are outside influences rather than our own ideas, we can renounce their assaults and not partner with them.

CHAPTER EIGHT

DISCERNING ATMOSPHERES

Over the past twenty years, I have seen thousands of people freed from lies and demonic strongholds. No matter how strong the enemy's presence feels, God's power always dispels its authority. I have found this to be true in the shifting of atmospheres as well.

I find this premise of displacement works well with shifting atmospheres. To work toward this, we must first develop our skills of *identification*. That which is being broadcast from an atmosphere might be either obvious or veiled. It is important we understand we may need to increase our level of discernment in order to effectively label what we feel, sense, or hear. Fortunately, it is biblically legal to practice our gifts of discernment:

But solid food is for the mature, for those who have their powers of discernment trained by constant practice to distinguish good from evil (Hebrews 5:14).

> ## DISCERNMENT IS PERHAPS THE SINGLE MOST IMPORTANT TOOL RELATIVE TO SHIFTING ATMOSPHERES.

Although it may seem like some people just "get" what is going on around them, I guarantee you anyone far along in their gift of discernment has spent years of practice.

To begin discerning spirits, start paying attention to how you feel in different environments. Take notes, journal, and ask others how they experience these same places. Are you calm everywhere you go or are there places or people who make your skin crawl? Are there stores in your town or buildings that you love visiting because you feel accepted and cared for? All of these feelings may emanate from the spiritual atmospheres governing the area.

As mentioned in Chapter Seven, you will have more success discerning atmospheres if you do not agree or come under their influence. The healthier you are, the more effective you will be. Make sure to pray through any issues you face before starting your own journey working toward discerning atmospheres. Jesus describes this need for inner healing in Matthew:

Why do you see the speck that is in your brother's eye, but do not notice the log that is in your own eye? Or how can you say to your brother, "Let me take the speck out of your eye," when there is the log in your own eye? (Matthew 7:3-4)

Once healed, you will find it is much easier to pick up/discern broadcasts and atmospheres.

<hr />

Discernment is perhaps the single most important tool relative to shifting atmospheres. The Bible makes it clear discernment is a spiritual gift we should be pursuing (see 1 Cor. 12:10). It is part of wisdom personified:

I, wisdom, dwell with prudence, and I find knowledge and discretion (Proverbs 8:12).

The church has, to a degree, stepped away from the influence of discernment because unhealthy believers have concealed jealousy, suspicion, and control in the guise of true discernment. I also find that many believers tend to have a misunderstanding of what "loving others" actually means.

In much of the church, there is a misconception that love does not confront, and therefore we tolerate all forms of sin. While this topic is much too large to debate in these pages, it is important to note that Jesus never minced His words and He was love personified. He even confronted Peter, one of His closest friends, for allowing Satan to speak through him.

When we devalue truth, discernment is diminished in our lives.

> IN MUCH OF THE CHURCH, THERE IS A MISCONCEPTION THAT LOVE DOES NOT CONFRONT, AND THEREFORE WE TOLERATE ALL FORMS OF SIN.

Stephen De Silva, head of Prosperous Soul Ministries, explains a way to train yourself to discern atmospheres. In his manual *Prosperous Soul Foundations*, Stephen writes:

> Because we are in Christ, we have authority to displace powers of darkness and shift them [to] heavenly atmospheres. As we tune in and listen to the heart of God, it becomes easier to discern evil frequencies trying to fill our atmosphere. We can then be empowered to keep our focus on God's promises instead.[1]

Knowing what God says about you, your situation, and your city will help you recognize broadcasts that do not line up with His voice or His nature.

The most common way people pick up atmospheres is through their senses. Through sight, smell, taste, and even touch, people "feel" what goes on around them. Although many Christians would not at first say they feel spiritual dynamics around them, once they learn this concept of atmospheres, puzzle pieces begin falling into place. They start paying attention to the subtle shifts in their moods throughout the day. For many "feelers," the teaching of shifting atmospheres provides much-needed relief. Having been told their whole lives that they were either crazy or hormonal, these highly-discerning individuals now have language to describe their unique way of discerning.

I woke up one morning on a ministry trip in a really bad mood. I prayed and asked God for a better attitude. As I got ready, I found myself getting more and more frustrated. By the time I got down to breakfast, I was in a really irritable mood. I did not want to hurt my team's feelings, so I said, "Hey guys. I just want to warn you that I am feeling really hormonal so if I snap at you today, do not take it personally. It is not you."

As I looked around for my team's reactions, I did not see concern. What I felt, instead was annoyance. I asked them, "Is anyone else feeling irritable?"

"No!" came the loud response. *Ha ha*, I thought. I realized they, too were frustrated and probably picking up the atmospheres hovering over the region. I had our team ask God to forgive us for partnering with grumpiness and commanded it to leave. Instantly, our attitudes shifted.

One of my friends went shopping with her young son at a store that had just changed its bathroom policies. The new policy, catering to gender identity issues, allowed customers to choose the bathroom they wanted to use.

While shopping, her son stood up in the shopping cart and shouted, "I am a boy! Not a girl!" His mom looked around to see who her son was talking to only to realize there was no one else around. Her son was not addressing flesh and blood. He was addressing and declaring to the spiritual realm that was harassing him about his truth in his identity.

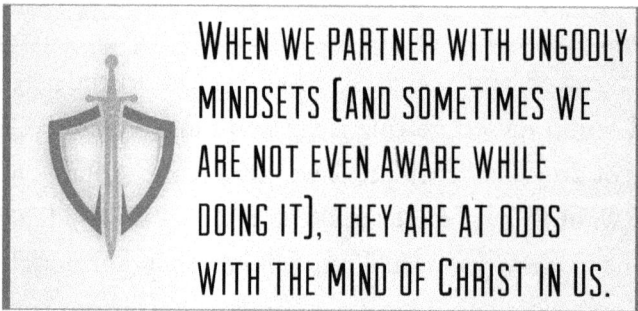

> WHEN WE PARTNER WITH UNGODLY MINDSETS (AND SOMETIMES WE ARE NOT EVEN AWARE WHILE DOING IT), THEY ARE AT ODDS WITH THE MIND OF CHRIST IN US.

One year, my team and I ministered in Australia. We had just finished a weekend seminar, and we and the local church team had enjoyed ourselves. We were leaving early the next morning, so we were transferred to a hotel in a city much nearer to the airport. This hotel was significantly older and quainter than the accommodations we had left behind; this also meant the hallways and guest rooms were smaller.

After our hosts dropped us off and checked in, we hauled our luggage up to our rooms. Only one of us at a time could fit in the elevator with our bags. Upon entering the lift, my heaviest suitcase rolled across my toes. While pulling it down the hallway, my bags bounced along the walls like some scattered game of ping pong. As I wedged myself into my hotel room, my coat pocket got stuck on the door handle and ripped a hole in my jacket. Needless to say, I had to bite my tongue to keep from spewing frustration all over the place.

After we were all situated, we grabbed dinner in a small restaurant across the street. We were seated right away but no one came to wait on us. After twenty minutes, the same irritation I had felt at the hotel began harassing me. Thoughts like *I can't believe they are ignoring us* and *wow, there goes their tip* filled my brain. As a Christian leader, I know not to give these thoughts a place in my mind. But in this moment, I struggled to take them captive.

I have always found it best to bring such thoughts out into the open, I took a deep breath and asked my team, "Is anyone else struggling with frustration?"

The team confirmed that they too were having some less than glamorous thoughts. As we tried to pin down the exact spirit we were listening to (so we could renounce it), Teresa Liebscher said, "We are in the business district."

"Ah-ha!" I said. "I've got it."

It turned out my team and I had been dealing with a spirit of entitlement. (Please note, I am not saying all business people carry a spirit of entitlement. This just happened to be the atmosphere settling in the region.) Not realizing this earlier, my team and I had begun partnering with its prevailing spirit and acting out accordingly. The broadcasts of entitlement released an *I deserve* message.

When we partner with ungodly mindsets (and sometimes we are not even aware while doing it), they are at odds with the mind of Christ in us. Instead of capturing these thoughts, we let them run their course. This frequently happens when we embrace the atmosphere's messages as our own.

Once my team and I realized we had been partnering with a spirit of entitlement, we asked God to forgive us. We repented for partnering with this *I deserve* attitude and repeated one of my favorite phrases, "We see you, spirit of entitlement. We are no longer going to partner with you, and we send you back in Jesus's name."

Instantly, we felt the spirit realm shift around us. Soon after, a waitress strolled over to take our orders and the rest of our dining experience was great.

⁘ ⸻ ⸻ ⁘

In this example, it took us a while to recognize that we were actually entertaining thoughts of an outside influence. This is not all that uncommon, even for those trained in the gift of discernment. Oftentimes, we are too busy or are so enjoying ourselves in "vacation mode" that we fail to accurately discern the surrounding atmospheres. This is why it is so important to surround ourselves with trusted accountability. If one person fails to discern the enemy's broadcasts, another will help:

> *Two are better than one, because they have a good reward for their toil. For if they fall, one will lift up his fellow. But woe to him who is alone when he falls and has not another to lift him up!* (Ecclesiastes 4:9-10)

Pay attention to the attitudes you experience throughout your day and partner with others in stewarding this increasing gift of discernment. Having another set of "spiritual eyes" will help you in moments when you fail to quickly detect the enemy's presence on your own.

It can be a challenge to find a mature prayer partner. I encourage people to find someone who is further along in their giftings. Partnering up with someone who has a stronger gift than you is an excellent way of expanding your own skills to the next level. I was blessed to find some great partners early on who helped me tremendously. Since then, we have built life-long friendships and continue to discuss our findings of the spiritual realm.

Another way to discern the atmospheres and spirits around you is to pay attention to the voices/messages you hear internally. As discussed in Chapter Seven, these voices usually mask themselves as your own thoughts. They typically appear in the first person with phrases like *I am*, *I can't*, or *I'm not*.

Sometimes, I hear an uncharacteristic phrase while praying for people. I pay attention to the wording because as unfamiliar phrases, they often signify the atmosphere the person is themselves emitting. Other times, it is the Holy Spirit teaching me how to confront a person's mindset.

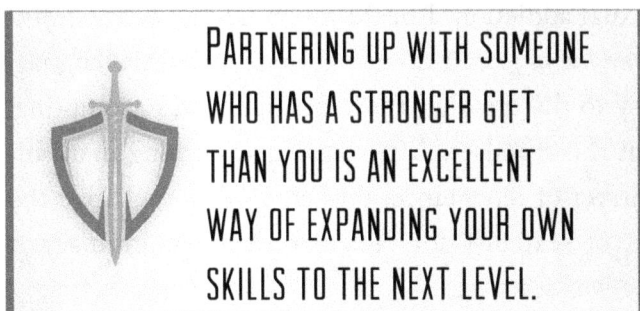

> PARTNERING UP WITH SOMEONE WHO HAS A STRONGER GIFT THAN YOU IS AN EXCELLENT WAY OF EXPANDING YOUR OWN SKILLS TO THE NEXT LEVEL.

Many times when people arrive for sessions, they come with a preconceived notion of how things will go. The two most common atmospheres people bring to the room as they come for prayer are hopelessness and discouragement. I have trained our teams to listen to the Holy Spirit's promptings and to discern the atmospheres the clients bring with them. After being trained in this, our teams can quickly dispel any atmospheres the client gives off and work to set them free from the corresponding mindsets.

One time, as a client entered my room he began to tell me that he was only coming to see me because his wife was being ministered to at the same time with another one of my team members in the next room. He did not feel like he needed to be ministered to because his wife (according to him) was the one who was truly messed up. As he continued to describe all the years of their marriage lost to her personal therapy, I heard the Holy Spirit say, *Ask him if he would like to deal with his loneliness.* When I asked him this, he stared at me in shock and asked, "How did you find that? I just told my wife that I felt lonely inside."

Another time while praying for a young man struggling with sexual addiction, I heard my mind say, *I can't help this guy. He has no moral grid.* I do not normally use this language, so it was easy to discern that the Holy Spirit was prompting me to confront this mindset. After leading the young man through a quick prayer of repentance, I asked God to exchange the man's mindset of sexuality for God's truth about intimacy. Shortly after, he was set free.

Sometimes the comments we hear in our minds while working with people are not promptings from the Holy Spirit but, instead, are spiritual broadcasts. I tell our Sozo team—if you fail to discern whether you are picking up your own or the client's spiritual broadcasts, you will agree with their struggles and not have authority over them.

One day, a man came in for his session. I had just finished with another person who had experienced tremendous freedom so I was confident this next man would also be set free. After shaking my hand, he said, "I don't see, I don't hear, and I don't feel. I have been prayed for by all the great ministers, and I am still broken."

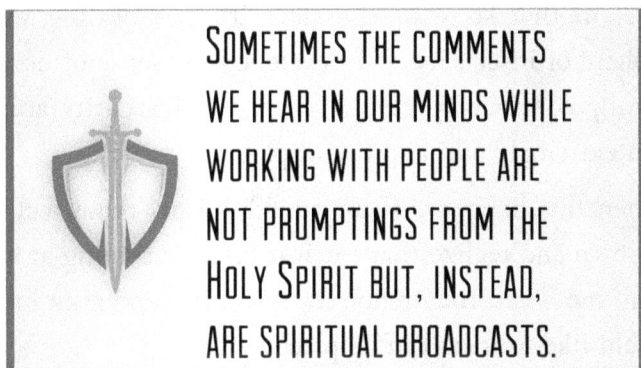

> SOMETIMES THE COMMENTS WE HEAR IN OUR MINDS WHILE WORKING WITH PEOPLE ARE NOT PROMPTINGS FROM THE HOLY SPIRIT BUT, INSTEAD, ARE SPIRITUAL BROADCASTS.

I was starting to feel a bit out of my league, so I tried encouraging myself and thought, *Well, at least he hasn't had a Sozo yet.* As soon as I had finished this thought, he blurted out, "And just in case you think Sozo is any better, I have already had three and none of them worked."

I was either going to win or lose this session right there. I heard my mind say, *Great. Thank You, Jesus. You sent me the one person on the planet even You can't heal!* Instead of agreeing with this thought, I heard myself say, "Great. Then I cannot let you down."

He looked at me, confused, and said, "What do you mean?"

I answered, "We can only go up from here."

He chuckled. In this small moment, he broke agreement with the atmosphere of hopelessness. Soon after, we were able to connect him to God for his freedom.

Many times, we hear thoughts or experience feelings while engaging in normal life. For instance, if I feel confident but walk into a drug store and begin to feel insecure, chances are someone in that store or the store itself is dealing with an atmosphere of insecurity. If I developed my sense of normal as a naturally confident person, thoughts of insecurity are going to seem extremely odd and out of place.

When this happens, I can quickly dispel these feelings as not my own and realize that the insecurity is coming at me and not from me. I can then renounce insecurity and ask God what He would like to install in its place.

Atmospheres in stores or buildings can be just as potent as those coming from individuals. A grocery store in my home-town is an example of this. For years, every time I returned from this specific store, I found myself with extra cans of chili and corn. When my husband asked why I bought so many, I simply answered, "They were on sale."

It did not seem to matter that I never really needed them. I always came home with more. Curious about this impulse, I started paying attention to how I felt when entering the store. Sure enough, every time I walked by the rows of canned chili,

I heard my brain scream, *What a great buy! I know I don't really need these but why not buy a few.*

As I continued to listen throughout the years, I noticed the store's underlying message of *buy me—you really need to buy me.*

Although this sounds absurd, you would be surprised how many people confirm my findings. They also hear the same voice calling to them while strolling down this specific aisle. Once, when I was in Norway and jokingly sharing this story, the translator, who had lived in Redding for years, stopped me mid-sentence and shouted, "I know what store that is! I've heard it too."

Months later, while lecturing at a drug and alcohol rehab class, I found myself retelling this story. Just when my brain was saying, *Wow. These guys are gonna want to ask you for the drugs you are on,* one of the students shouted, "Is it this store?"

When I said yes, he said, "That makes so much sense. I shop at that store and wonder why I always buy so many cans of chili."

Years later, I met a man who had actually worked at that store. He said the managers always told him to stock the shelves so that the "Cans would call out to the customers as they passed by."

Some people actually see angels and demons intervening as well as sense or hear the atmosphere's broadcasts. These people are called *seers* and possess a unique spiritual gift that allows them to see into both the physical and spiritual realm. It is far more common to see pictures internally in your mind rather than externally like an open vision. Both can be powerful. Dreaming is one of the most common ways this gift manifests.

Years ago, our flight had just landed in the U.K. That night, in my hotel room, I tossed and turned to wake myself up from a series of violent nightmares. In each one, I woke myself up right before being raped. This continued throughout the night. The next day, I went to my son's, Tim's, door and knocked. He answered it rather sleepily.

"Ha!" I said, "You've got jet lag!"

"It's not that, Mom." He said. "All night long I dreamt I was rescuing women from being raped."

My eyes widened. During the night, we had picked up the atmosphere over that city of sexual violence; now we could strategize with the church leaders on how to reverse its hold.

The next day, we partnered with the street pastors and released atmospheres of honor and protection to displace perversion, addiction, and violation. Since our visit, the city has seen a drastic decline in sexual violence.

Sometimes, it is possible to smell the spiritual realm. While I have heard Christians saying Jesus is sweet and lovely, I have so far only been able to smell demonic activity. One time One time, while teaching at a seminar, I noticed a terrible rotten-egg smell. My first thought was, *Wow, someone has really bad gas,* so I moved to the other side of the stage. No matter where I moved, the scent followed. About an hour into my teaching, the scent finally faded. I took a deep breath of relief. After my session ended, I left the stage and sat with my intercessor friend, Renee.

"Did you smell anything while I was on stage?" I asked.

"Yes," she said. "There were three snakes behind you on stage. But don't worry, I took care of them."

> WE NEED TO BE ABLE TO DISCERN BETWEEN GOOD AND EVIL, BECAUSE MANY TIMES THE ENEMY WILL TRY TO MIMIC WHAT GOD IS DOING.

Another time, I was on a trip to Tennessee. We explored the World's Fair buildings that were replicas of famous structures. As we were walking into the Parthenon, I smelled the same scent that assaulted me every time I went to the hospitals to pray for the sick. Until then, I thought it was the combination of human waste, body fluids, and cleaning supplies. I thought, *How is this possible that I am smelling it here?* I heard the Lord respond, *It is the spirit of death.*

A good friend of mine visited her ailing mother at the hospital weeks later. Her mother had been ill on and off for several years, but this time the doctors told her to gather the family to say their goodbyes. As she walked into the room, she smelled the smell of death and remembered my earlier comment. She rebuked the spirit and told it to move aside so that all her family members could arrive and say their goodbyes. Her mother rallied back and was coherent for the next few days while all the family got to spend precious time with her before she passed.

At times, you can experience physical sensations that come from the spiritual realm. Such sensations can make you feel instantly hot or unnaturally cold. The sensation you feel can sometimes give you a clue about the presence of a nearby spirit. Changes in body temperature, however, are not always signs of demonic activity. It can also be a way to experience the power of God. Many times in sessions and on the prayer lines, people feel heat or extreme cold in affected areas of their body.

This is why we must grow in our levels of discernment. We need to be able to discern between good and evil, because many times the enemy will try to mimic what God is doing. This is done so the enemy can spread confusion or fear.

As you pay attention to the spiritual atmospheres around you, you will notice that patterns form. For me, it is when I am in an area with strong witchcraft ties; my body begins to experience vertigo. When my back just below my left shoulder blade feels like it is being stabbed, it is usually an indication of someone cursing or talking bad about me. When I am around controlling people, I get very tired and have to fight falling asleep. I have learned these signs are "tells" for me, so when they occur I can easily discern what is going on around me and take authority over it.

Find someone to begin practicing discerning atmospheres with you. Make a list of how you feel and what you hear internally as you move throughout your day. You may want to pick up my workbook, *Atmospheres 101*, to get you started.

NOTE

1. De Silva, *Prosperous Soul Foundations*.

CHAPTER NINE

SHIFTING ATMOSPHERES

Take no part in the unfruitful works of darkness,
but instead expose them. For it is shameful even
to speak of the things that they do in secret. But
when anything is exposed by the light, it becomes
visible, for anything that becomes visible is light.
Therefore it says, "Awake, O sleeper, and arise
from the dead, and Christ will shine on you."
—EPHESIANS 5:11-14

*S*hine in this verse is from the word *epiphausei*, which means "to shine upon or give light to."[1] As followers of Christ we have a mandate to let our light so shine as to bring glory to God:

> *Nor do people light a lamp and put it under a basket, but on a stand, and it gives light to all in the house. In the same way, let your light shine before others, so that they may see your good works and give glory to your Father who is in heaven* (Matthew 5:15-16).

Shifting atmospheres is a way to shine in such a way that you draw people to the one true God. We should be walking transmitters of His character and release His attributes into every atmosphere we encounter.

Jesus referred to Himself as the light of the world, and John later stated:

> *God is light, and in him is no darkness at all* (1 John 1:5).

As I write this, I am reminded of a session I facilitated recently that resonates with Matthew 5:16. A woman came in to see me to try and discover why she continually self-sabotaged her efforts for weight loss. She explained that during the day, she did really well with her dieting plan, but at night she would self-sabotage by gorging on snacks. I asked the Lord to show her the root cause of this. As a result, God took her back to a memory of when she was thirteen years old.

In this memory, she had finally managed the courage to expose the sexual abuse that was rampant in her home for the past several years. After bringing the family's sin into the light, her mother completely shut down and stopped talking to her. In her memory, she was in the kitchen at night grabbing Oreo cookies and a glass of milk when she turned and saw her mother ignoring her in the living room. She bravely asked, "Why won't you just talk to me?"

Her mom said, "I will when you apologize for having an affair with my husband."

She felt this was absolutely ridiculous, so she simply grabbed the cookies and milk and headed back to her room instead of apologizing.

Once she forgave her mom in our session and told her body it did not have to carry her mother's shame any more, a demonic presence flew out of her chest and knocked me back in my chair as it left. Immediately, the room got brighter. In this example, a demonic spirit was partially hiding her "light" through its residence in her life (see Matt. 5:14-16).

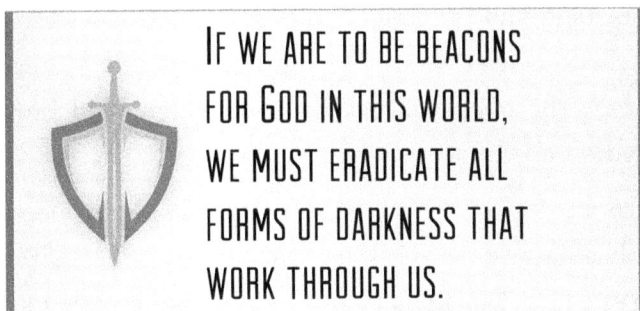

> IF WE ARE TO BE BEACONS FOR GOD IN THIS WORLD, WE MUST ERADICATE ALL FORMS OF DARKNESS THAT WORK THROUGH US.

I was once in a deliverance conference where the lecturer was telling a similar story. A pastor had called his friend to come pray for his church because the past four pastors had fallen into sexual sin. He did not feel like he himself had any open doors, but his wife felt a strong conviction from the Holy Spirit to see if the church was housing a spirit of perversion.

While the pastor and his friend prayed through his church building room by room, they sensed an evil presence in one of the lower basement classrooms. After repenting for the prior leaders' partnerships with this spirit, they commanded it to leave and invited the Holy Spirit.

The next morning after service, several members of the congregation confronted the head pastor: why had he not asked them to help paint the inside of the church? They remarked how the church seemed so much brighter, and he could not convince them that he had not painted the walls.

If we are to be beacons for God in this world, we must eradicate all forms of darkness that work through us. Our homes should be peaceful and our neighborhoods safe. Our businesses should be the friendliest and most profitable. When we understand and properly shift atmospheres, we strategically release the nature of Jesus. By imparting heaven's broadcasts, we become the open heavens through which God broadcasts His virtues into the world.

Once we realize we are picking up outside influences, we can easily renounce ties with them. When you identify the spirit you are sensing, you expose it to the light and cripple its power. Many times, a simple declaration is sufficient for shifting the atmospheres around you. What follows is a sample declaration:

I see you [fill in whichever atmosphere you are discerning]. I am not partnering with you and I send you back.

This declaration is a starting point for you to begin practicing your discernment and spiritual authority. If you want to shift atmospheres for others as well as yourself, you will need to do a bit more work.

After you discern an atmosphere, your next step is to ask the Lord what opposing message He wishes to impart in its place. I use the word "opposing" because Satan is always working against the things of God. If the Lord wants to restore peace, prosperity, and unity, then the devil will most likely be broadcasting messages of chaos, poverty, and offense.

If you partner with a prevailing spirit in any way, you will need to ask God to forgive you before you move on to the next phase of displacement. Doing so realigns you with the nature of God and covers you with His grace. God's forgiveness repositions us under His wings where we are kept safe from the enemy—and this is powerfully shown in one of my favorite psalms:

> *He who dwells in the shelter of the Most High will abide in the shadow of the Almighty. I will say to the Lord, "My refuge and my fortress, my God, in whom I trust!" For it is He who delivers you from the snare of the trapper and from the deadly pestilence. He will cover you with His pinions, and under His wings you may seek refuge; His faithfulness is a shield and bulwark. You will not be afraid of the terror by night, or of the arrow that flies by day; of the pestilence that stalks in darkness, or of the destruction that lays waste at noon. A thousand may fall at your side and ten*

thousand at your right hand, but it shall not approach you (Psalm 91:1-7 NASB).

> ## AFTER YOU DISCERN AN ATMOSPHERE, YOUR NEXT STEP IS TO ASK THE LORD WHAT OPPOSING MESSAGE HE WISHES TO IMPART IN ITS PLACE.

When you are engaged in spiritual warfare, make sure you are in the shelter of the Most High.

As we stand in the gap for ourselves and others, we partner with God's mercy to deliver the oppressed—even if we are technically not oppressed ourselves. There is something powerful in humbling ourselves before the Lord and offering ourselves to His will that activates us with His power, covering, and victory.

Repentance is not just saying we're sorry but is also an acknowledgment that our actions were not in line with God's. When we ask God to forgive us for partnering with a specific spirit, we acknowledge both our wrongful actions as well as our intentions to refrain from them. The powerful response of God to our repentance is the very nature of grace.

Once we identify and renounce the broadcasts and work through repentance, we are ready to begin shifting the atmospheres. This is the step of displacement. It is done by replacing the enemy's schemes with God's truth. To clarify the difference between renouncing and replacing, view the following chart below for some examples:

FEELING	RENOUNCING	REPLACING
JEALOUS	"I see/sense you, jealousy, I am not partnering with you, and I send you back in Jesus's name."	"Forgive me, Father, for partnering with jealousy. As You forgive me, I invite You to release humility and acceptance into this atmosphere."
ANXIOUS	"I see/sense you, fear, and I will not partner with you. I send you back in Jesus's name."	"Forgive me, Father, for partnering with fear. I invite You, Holy Spirit, to come and release Your peace into this place."
HOPELESS	"I see/sense you, hopelessness. I am not partnering with you and I send you back in Jesus's name."	"Forgive me, Father, for partnering with hopelessness. I hand You any lies I am believing that partner with this broadcast. I invite You to fill me and this atmosphere with hope, expectation, and faith."
PERVERSION/ SEXUAL SIN	"I see/sense you, perversion, and I send you back in Jesus's name."	"Forgive me, Father, for any agreements I have made with sexual sin. I invite You to come and release purity into the atmosphere."

FEELING	RENOUNCING	REPLACING
CONFUSION	*"I see/sense you, confusion, and I renounce you in Jesus's name."*	*"Forgive me, Father, for partnering with confusion. I invite You to release clarity, peace, and order in its place."*
ANGER/ RAGE	*"I see/sense you, anger, and I am not going to be counseled by you. I send you back in Jesus's name."*	*"Father, forgive me for agreeing with anger. May the gifts of love, peace, kindness, patience, and self-control invade this atmosphere."*
SADNESS/ DEPRESSION	*"I see/sense you, sadness. I am not partnering with you. I send you back in Jesus's name."*	*"Father, I ask You to forgive me for letting sadness and depression steal my joy. Your joy is my strength, so I ask You to release it in this place."*

These prayers are not to be seen as formulas but as examples of ways to pray. As we pick up the broadcasts of the enemy and reject them, we will need to inquire of God what He wants us to release. Many times, I find it is the opposite of what I have been picking up. Other times, He has very specific strategies for what to release into the atmosphere. What's important is to listen to Him and release what He wants us to pray.

Months ago as I was teaching in North Carolina, my team and I kept sensing a spirit of poverty over the area. Instead of sensing that God wanted us to pray and battle against poverty directly, I felt the Holy Spirit prompting us to publicly honor the assistant pastor and his family for all their hard work over the years. At the same time, Teresa sensed that we needed to ask God to release His angels over the church. When I asked her how to do this, she shrugged and said, "I don't know. You're in charge. You get to figure it out."

I had no idea how to cooperate with God to see His angels released. All I had was this prompting to honor the assistant pastor. After getting permission from the head pastor, we brought up the assistant pastor with his family Sunday morning and had them stand in front of the congregation. I spoke to the audience, who were mostly college students, and said, "All week long you have been telling me how much you love this guy. So I am giving you an opportunity to put your money where your mouth is and come show him how much you love him."

Our team started the rush by bringing their offerings. Immediately, the congregation sprang out of their seats and brought cash, stuffing it into the family's hands and pockets until the money overflowed out onto the ground. As this was happening, we felt a shift occurring over this family and within the church. When the family got home and counted all the money, the youngest son said, "Dad, when people came up and began placing money in our hands, I saw the doors of the church open and a bunch of angels came in and lined up along the walls."

Who could have guessed that honoring this family publicly would release the presence of angels? Needless to say, a tangible economic shift took place over both this family and the church. I have been told it still holds today.

> ### LISTEN TO HIM AND RELEASE WHAT HE WANTS US TO PRAY.

Shifting atmospheres can occur on a personal, regional, or national scale. We will examine more closely how to shift some of these atmospheres in subsequent chapters. We need to recognize, however, that the higher you go in terms of scale, the more powerful the demonic spirits you encounter. I find it unwise to take on a principality or ruler (higher level demons) alone or even directly. Be sure to partner with the Holy Spirit and stay under the shelter of the Most High.

We were never designed to agree with the devil's works. We can empathize with those we pray with but should never allow our sympathy to outweigh our ability to come above the devil's attacks. Cory learned this well while ministering in New Zealand.

We had been invited to a new church and were asked to work with individuals who sought inner healing. Cory received one client, a middle-aged woman, who shared about her struggles with neck pain. Sometimes it was so severe she had to lay down for several hours until it passed. After praying with the Holy Spirit, Cory realized that this pain was not merely coincidental. It was the direct result of demonic oppression.

It turns out her husband was involved in cult practices that opened a door to the demonic. Even though she was saved, this opening allowed unclean spirits to take advantage of her life, which eventually gave way to fear and spiritual attacks. Before long, she was experiencing mood swings so violent that her husband (also demonically oppressed) asked her to seek help. Six months later, she sat in a small room with her father and Cory to work through these issues.

When asked when these neck pains started, she revealed the dark patterns in her life that brought about her anger. Her husband was himself a rager, so she resorted to what she thought was strength (rage) to stand up to his violence. As they worked through these issues, Cory asked the Holy Spirit if there was anything else demonic in this area that needed to be addressed.

After this woman, Mary, was asked to repeat a prayer, she began to twitch uncontrollably. Her voice lowered several octaves. Obviously, the demon that oppressed her spirit was taking over. Unfazed, Cory retaliated with his favorite weapon—joy. While laughing off the demon's approach, he invited the Holy Spirit's presence. Instantly, the demon left. There was no competition. Mary, blinking as if awakened from a trance, looked at Cory and told him that her neck pain was gone.

> BE SURE TO PARTNER WITH THE HOLY SPIRIT AND STAY UNDER THE SHELTER OF THE MOST HIGH.

The most encouraging aspect of this story is how quickly the evil spirit left. Once the Holy Spirit invaded, there was no competition. Mary renounced her partnership with sin and handed over to Jesus the access it had to her. She left the room both physically and emotionally healed as well as delivered. Such is the power of the God in our lives. No matter how strong the enemy appears, he is no match for the Lord:

> Then he said to them, "Go your way. Eat the fat and drink sweet wine and send portions to anyone who has nothing ready, for this day is holy to our Lord. And do not be grieved, for the joy of the Lord is your strength" (Nehemiah 8:10).

Mary's story is an example of when it is fairly easy to renounce partnership with an evil spirit. Some deliverances (personal shiftings of atmospheres) might take more time depending on the hierarchy of the demon and number of strongholds in a person's life. Eventually though, when an inferior kingdom comes into contact with a greater one, the weaker will fall.

> NO MATTER HOW STRONG THE ENEMY APPEARS, HE IS NO MATCH FOR THE LORD.

One example of how *not* to deal with atmospheres was experienced by Cory while on a ministry trip to Scotland. He and his brother, Tim, stayed in the upstairs room of an old cottage. Each night, Cory experienced nightmares. He later recounted how he saw a demon in his room each night but because of his lack of discernment training he shrugged it off as imagination.

Later, he discerned this demon was actually a spirit of fear. But there was another spirit suffusing the room, unknown to Cory but correctly discerned by Tim—anger.

Days before, when Tim and Cory first entered the room, Tim's seer eyes perceived the spirit lounging on his bed, and it told him, "This is my place. You are not welcome."

Undeterred, Tim plopped his bags on the bed and said, "Yeah, well, you better move 'cause I'm ready for a nap."

The demon recognized Tim's impenetrable confidence, so it left and moved on to bother Cory instead. While we can laugh at it now, my oldest son did not handle the situation as well.

By the last night, Cory was being harassed so badly that he decided to check with his brother to see if these "figments of his imagination" were real. Lying in bed, Cory turned to his brother.

"Tim."

"Yeah?"

"Have you felt anything creepy in this room?"

"Yep."

"You have?"

"And we're not gonna talk about it."

Up to this point, Cory's strategy had been *It's ok, he'll say no. He'll prove there are no demons in this lodge, and we'll brush things off and move on with normal life.* But Tim's response startled Cory, whose previously held belief that demons were real but rarely interfered with our affairs was broken. Staring up at the unlit ceiling, Cory witnessed the darkness get darker. A feeling of suffocation swept over him. Immediately, everything he had come to believe about the spiritual realm was shattered.

At this point, Cory made an even greater mistake. Having identified the presence of the demons, he did not renounce their presence. Instead, he partnered with them by giving in to their harassments. Tim, on the other hand, started singing worship songs and invited the Lord's presence. In the meantime, Cory cowered beneath his blankets and witnessed visions of angels and demons swirling over his cottage. After what felt like hours, Cory finally fell to sleep.

In the morning, Cory and Tim descended the stairs. Tim looked comfortably rested, but Cory was obviously still fatigued. In truth, he had not slept well at all. As we found out, he had been battling demons all night long. On the way to the airport, Cory poked his head between the front seats of the car.

"You mind brushing me off?" he said. "I feel slimed."

I looked back over my shoulder and gave him the routine clean-up inspection.

"That's because there's a demon on your shoulder," I said.

"There's a what?!" Cory jumped back.

"No, worries. Tim will get it off."

Tim reached over and brushed Cory's shoulder, saying, "In Jesus's name, I brush off the spirit of *chaos!*"

Upon saying "chaos," the spirit leapt off Cory's shoulder and flew out of the car, raising Tim up along the way as he hit his scalp on the ceiling of the car. Tim began rubbing his head while Cory, meanwhile, sank down into his seat, relieved.

"Thanks," he said. "I feel better."

Tim massaged his skull and looked over at his brother with horror.

"What happened to you last night?"

Many times, we learn as much if not more from our failed attempts than from our successes. In this humorous and educational encounter, Cory learned a few things. He is now more relaxed when confronted with demonic spirits and his confidence of knowing who he is in Christ makes him a much more powerful warrior.

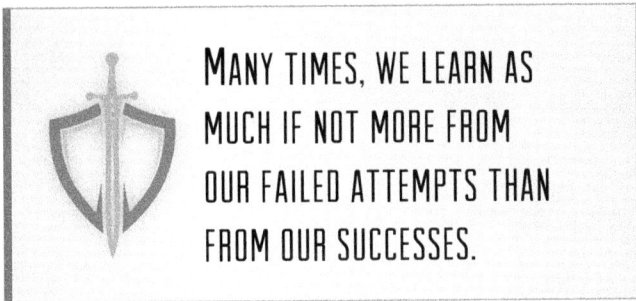

> MANY TIMES, WE LEARN AS MUCH IF NOT MORE FROM OUR FAILED ATTEMPTS THAN FROM OUR SUCCESSES.

Cory's above experience is a semi-comical example of how not to partner with evil spirits. When we see, hear, or come into contact with them, we are first and foremost not to give in to fear. Tim's victory happened because he was confident in his authority. When the enemy tried to intimidate him, he simply rejected it. Cory, on the other hand, partnered with fear and allowed its false authority to harass him.

———————

I hope this story encourages you in your own walk. Realize that when you come into contact with or are attacked by the enemy, it is not God's way of punishing you. Use these attacks to train yourself to grow your spiritual authority and allow the Holy Spirit to give you strategies so you can emerge victorious.

NOTE

1. Blue Letter Bible, s.v. "Epiphauskō," February 12, 2017, https://www.blueletterbible.org/lang/lexicon/lexicon.cfm ?Strongs=G2017&t=ESV.

CHAPTER TEN

SHIFTING ATMOSPHERES OVER YOURSELF AND YOUR HOME

And God blessed them, and God said unto them,
Be fruitful, and multiply, and replenish the earth,
and subdue it; and have dominion over the fish
of the sea, and over the fowl of the air, and over
every living thing that moveth upon the earth.
—GENESIS 1:28, KJV

Behold, I have given you authority to tread on
serpents and scorpions, and over all the power
of the enemy, and nothing shall hurt you.
—LUKE 10:19

The word *dominion* in Genesis 1:28 means "to rule, have dominion, dominate, and tread down."[1] Just as God commanded Adam and Eve to have dominion over the fish of the sea, the birds of the air, and beasts of the field, so too has He given us authority over all the powers of the enemy. We are to exert this authority over our own lives, homes, cities, and regions.

Part of wielding our authority comes through the declarations we make and the actions that follow these declarations. Jesus instructed His disciples to release the good news into the atmospheres wherever they went and to match these declarations with action:

> *And proclaim as you go, saying, "The kingdom of heaven is at hand." Heal the sick, raise the dead, cleanse lepers, cast out demons. You received without paying; give without pay* (Matthew 10:7-8).

The word for *proclaim* in this verse translates as "to proclaim loudly as heralds."[2] The disciples were literally told to shout loudly as they journeyed through cities—declaring that the Kingdom of heaven was near. In addition, they were told to prove their claims through the demonstration of signs and wonders. This assignment has not been revoked.

> PART OF WIELDING OUR AUTHORITY COMES THROUGH THE DECLARATIONS WE MAKE AND THE ACTIONS THAT FOLLOW THESE DECLARATIONS.

The first part of this verse is an example of how one seeds truth into the atmosphere. This truth, tuned into and received by others, becomes a reality that others can step into. As I go throughout my day, I consider—what am I seeding into the atmosphere? When people are near me, what reality am I offering?

The goal of shifting atmospheres is not just to fix your city, region, or home but also to learn how to steward your own broadcasts. This starts with your heart:

> *But the things that come out of a person's mouth come from the heart, and these defile them* (Matthew 15:18 NIV).

> *Above all else, guard your heart, for everything you do flows from it* (Proverbs 4:23 NIV).

We guard our hearts by stewarding what we allow into them. When we evaluate what flows out from our hearts, we recalibrate ourselves so that the next outflow more resembles Christ. This is the basis of stewardship:

> *And the Lord said, "Who then is the faithful and wise manager, whom his master will set over his household, to give them their portion of food at the proper time? Blessed is that servant whom his master will find so doing when he comes* (Luke 12:42-43).

A *steward* is someone who supervises arrangements, manages, or keeps order. God has entrusted us to keep order over this earth and to be good stewards. This call to stewardship also extends to our hearts.

You can shift the atmospheres over your heart by first identifying the mindsets that drive your actions. These mindsets are at the root of your "normal" and either sprout from a truth or lie that has been accepted in your life. If it is a lie, you must work with the Holy Spirit to uproot its influence.

Inner thoughts like *I can't trust anyone* and *no one likes me* are rooted in our past experiences. This is why many people who have been hurt in previous relationships have trouble opening up to others. Their inner beliefs, warped by pain, are broadcasted into the atmosphere. Soon people begin to pick up and respond to them.

Some examples of lies and their related mindsets are listed below:

LIE	MINDSET
"Everyone is against me."	Victim
"I have to fend for myself."	Orphan
"Success is achieved through sabotaging others."	Bully
"Someday I will win, but not today."	Resignation
"I will never succeed."	Hopelessness
"God does not care if I do this little sin."	Deception
"It is okay to lie a little to keep peace."	Manipulation
"I have to make sure people's intentions are favorable to me."	Control
"It is my job to make people happy."	Performance
"I am doing a better job than most of these other guys."	Pride
"I am a realist. The glass is half-empty, not half-full."	Pessimism

When we partner with ungodly mindsets, we allow their messages to be broadcast from our hearts. Pay attention to how people respond to you. If there is a pattern, it is quite possible they are simply responding to the messages you are releasing.

It is not enough to simply identify the mindset to reverse its effect. Freedom from these mindsets comes as we remove lies and exchange them for God's truth. As you take ownership over the lies in your heart and exchange them for God's revealed truth, the atmospheres you release will change. An encouraging verse for me is:

> *Let us not lose heart in doing good, for in due time we will reap if we do not grow weary* (Galatians 6:9 NASB).

Many times when my husband mentors people regarding their finances, he counsels them to stay on the path of sowing new "seed" (healthy habits) even before they begin to walk in the benefit of new fields. If you find yourself reaping an old harvest even after sowing new seed, take heart. Your new field will break forth and produce good fruit. It might just be one more step away.

> FREEDOM FROM THESE MINDSETS COMES AS WE REMOVE LIES AND EXCHANGE THEM FOR GOD'S TRUTH.

In my own life, my struggles with judgment and criticism made it impossible for me to meet new people without instantly sizing them up. My internal Pharisee discerned the things these people were dealing with and I gladly partnered with judgment in order to protect myself from them.

Instead of interceding on their behalf, I relegated them to either safe or unsafe categories of people. When the Lord healed my fear of being hurt by others, I was able to break agreement with judgment and forsake partnership with a Pharisee mindset. People who knew me both before and after the breakthrough were stunned at the change in my demeanor.

In my case, a judging mindset and critical spirit took root in my heart and seeped out into the atmosphere around me. Even though I tried being a good Christian, I still broadcasted ungodly messages of aloofness and criticism that others picked up on and responded to.

If you feel a mindset is transmitting ungodly atmospheres from you, ask the Holy Spirit to reveal the lies you are believing. Simple prayers like the ones below may be all it takes for discovery:

1. Holy Spirit, would you reveal to me any ungodly atmospheres I am giving off?

2. Holy Spirit, what mindsets am I believing that manifest in this atmosphere?

3. Show me the lies, Holy Spirit, I am believing that make up this mindset.

4. Who do I need to forgive for first teaching me these lies?

5. What truth do You want to give me to replace these lies with?

6. Thank You, Holy Spirit, for healing my heart. I plant Your truths deep inside my heart so I can begin to transmit healthy atmospheres.

If you need to work through more lies and mindsets, I suggest you seek personal inner healing. You will learn how to walk through your own inner healing as you partner with God to expose lies, heal wounds, and release truth. The more you steward wholeness into your heart, the easier it will be not to partner with atmospheres that reflect your own inner wounds.

Once we fix our own broadcasts, we can begin to shift the atmospheres in our homes. Wherever your *home* exists—in the suburbs or the country, in a wealthy or developing area—realize God has placed you there for a purpose. Like pieces on a chess board, God has strategically placed you to contribute to His design. Your home, the environment from which your family operates, is your control center in shifting atmospheres. Think of it as your base of operations.

Our homes, rented or owned, are physical manifestations of the spiritual territory we possess. When friends, family, and other guests enter our homes, they should literally step into a God experience. This is much like when the Queen of Sheba visited King Solomon, tested his wisdom, and experienced how he outwardly expressed his inner atmosphere. She was left breathless (see 2 Chron. 9:3-4).

We are told what to think, believe, and embrace as normal through our media, education, and government. Agendas of *perversion*, *misinformation*, and *division* work to tear apart the family unit. These are just some of the worldly leaven being broadcasted through certain societal venues. We must be careful of what we allow into our home environments. Everything we bring in, good or bad, affects our atmosphere.

> # YOUR HOME, THE ENVIRONMENT FROM WHICH YOUR FAMILY OPERATES, IS YOUR CONTROL CENTER IN SHIFTING ATMOSPHERES.

Years ago when my boys were very young, the Lord began to convict me of the entertainment we allowed our kids to watch. At first, I was confused because I felt we regulated their cartoons and movies very well. The Lord, however, kept prompting me to take a look at what my boys were watching, so I laid out all our Disney movies and asked God which ones we should keep.

I ended up throwing away nearly half of the Disney movies we owned as the Lord prompted me, even though it was not easy for me to do. At the time, we did not have a lot of money and these movies were not cheap. It was also hard on my kids because they did not understand why they could not watch some of their favorite characters. Looking back, I should have invited my family to pray with me about which movies to keep.

I was vindicated, however, one day when my kids and I went to drop off groceries for our friends. We had just gone shopping, and I had put aside one of every "two for one bargains" I had been able to purchase. One was assigned to our family. The other was for our friends in need. Again, it was at the time in our lives when we ourselves had very little income.

On the way to drop off some food, my boys began to complain about not being able to watch *Aladdin* any more.

I told them, "I'm sorry, guys, but I just don't feel like we should celebrate him being a thief."

"But Mom," they chimed in. "He is not all bad. He turns out good. Besides, what he steals he shares with poor people."

I thought for a moment, then heard the Holy Spirit say through me, "Should our friends steal food to eat, or should we help provide for them?"

I am sure my boys still missed their shows, but they never complained about it again. In fact, I overheard them many times telling their friends, "No, we're not allowed to watch that one."

I will set no worthless thing before my eyes (Psalm 101:3 NASB).

To see the complete transformation and change within society, we must take ownership over our own homes. Once God sees us as trustworthy servants, He entrusts us with more.

When we look to create a safe environment in our homes, we must ask—*what does a healthy atmosphere in a marriage, home, or family look like?*

If a family follows Jesus and partners with the Holy Spirit, the atmospheres in their home should reflect *love, peace, acceptance, contentment, trust,* and *connection.* When a husband and wife partner together and install heavenly atmospheres over their lives, the hearts of their children and their home should reflect a healthy, similar quality.

Over the years, we have had many people help out around the house—cleaners, gardeners, and handymen. Our cleaner continues to tell us how much she loves working in our home because she feels so much peace. We have also lost many handymen over the years because after they started working for us they began to prosper in their businesses. They became too busy to continue pampering us. They stepped into and came under the covering of our home's spiritual atmosphere—peace and prosperity.

> ## TO SEE THE COMPLETE TRANSFORMATION AND CHANGE WITHIN SOCIETY, WE MUST TAKE OWNERSHIP OVER OUR OWN HOMES.

When a family fails to partner with Jesus and the Holy Spirit, atmospheres like *hostility, suspicion, bitterness, fear, disconnection,* or *sexual impurity* may develop. The Christian home should be a representation of God's Kingdom on earth. Just as Father God provides *protection, provision,* and *security* for His children, so should earthly fathers provide a safe spiritual, emotional, and physical environment for their families. The father's authority should not be wielded for abuse, manipulation, or control. Healthy fathers bring stability to the home rather than fear and control. Jesus said:

> *You know that the rulers of the Gentiles lord it over them, and their great ones exercise authority over them. It shall not be so among you. But whoever would be great among you must be your servant, and whoever would be first among you must be your slave, even as the Son of Man came not to be served but to serve, and to give his life as a ransom for many* (Matthew 20:25-28).

Paul echoed this in Ephesians when he encouraged husbands to love their wives even to the point of death:

> *Husbands, love your wives, as Christ loved the church and gave himself up for her, that he might sanctify her, having cleansed her by the washing of water with the word, so that he might present the church to himself in splendor, without spot or wrinkle or any such thing, that she might be holy and without blemish* (Ephesians 5:25-27).

Wives, like the Holy Spirit, are designed to be *helpers, instructors,* and *comforters.* Given the important task of bearing and rearing children, it is a woman's call to see the next generation brought up in truth, health, and wholeness. This is more easily attained when the home is united as a place of safety, encouragement, and love.

In the modern world, it is sometimes uncomfortable to talk about women as helpers rather than powerful forces to be reckoned with. Any mother, however, can tell you she has been a powerful force for her family. When the family unit works as designed, all members of the household are respected and thrive. A great teaching on this is Stephen De Silva's "The World's Tallest Man."[3]

Sometimes, people skew verses to promote their own theology regarding the family unit. This is particularly true in the case of women. Many have used the following verse as an excuse to exercise control and dominance, even to the point of physical, emotional, and sexual abuse.

> *Wives, submit to your own husbands, as to the Lord.*
> *For the husband is the head of the wife even as Christ*
> *is the head of the church, his body, and is himself its*
> *Savior. Now as the church submits to Christ, so also*
> *wives should submit in everything to their husbands*
> (Ephesians 5:22-24).

Rather than use this verse as an excuse to suppress women, I see it as a strategy to keep conflict out of the house by imparting an atmosphere of mutual respect. Just as the Holy Spirit is sent alongside us to minister and guide us, so do wives and mothers provide encouragement and support. I personally do not feel any less significant than my husband, for we are one flesh. Our ability to run our home with confidence (knowing that he is for me and I am for him) removes ecosystems of distrust and replaces them with environments of peace.

> WHEN THE FAMILY UNIT
> WORKS AS DESIGNED, ALL
> MEMBERS OF THE HOUSEHOLD
> ARE RESPECTED AND THRIVE.

God wants our relationships and homes to be healthy. We must follow the roadmaps provided us by Scripture and solidify the bonds among our neighbors, spouses, children, and leaders. When a husband and wife partner in peace and unity, heavenly atmospheres are released. If a couple embraces fear, discouragement, abuse, or strife, demonic atmospheres invade the home. Fear and anger become governing ecosystems that leak from our homes into the community. Our home base is truly a strategic fortress for shifting the community's atmospheres.

When a husband and wife partner with the Holy Spirit to raise their children in accordance with biblical values, atmospheres of love, joy, peace, patience, goodness, kindness, longsuffering, and self-control develop. These atmospheres become their children's normal that they gravitate toward throughout their lives. I believe this baseline created by a family's home life is what is described in Proverbs:

> *Train up a child in the way he should go; even when he is old he will not depart from it* (Proverbs 22:6).

If you want to shift atmospheres in your home, set up a family meeting to decide together what atmospheres you want released in your home. Once you agree on what you want your home to "feel like," then pray and ask the Holy Spirit for family strategies to accomplish your goals. You will find that there are some things your family needs to stop doing and others they need to begin. Make a list together so you can hold each other accountable; do not be offended when your children confront you if you revert to an old pattern.

Be careful not to use this strategy as a way to punish family members. We want this to be fun and effective. Remember that we are practicing and rarely get it right all the time. Partner with the grace of God as your family works to shift atmospheres and release His Kingdom.

Several years ago, I experienced a very stressful time period in my life. Tim was in elementary school, Cory in junior high, and I was the full-time finance manager at their Christian school as well as the high school Spanish teacher. (Can you feel the frenzy already?) But wait, there is more. My stepmother had just passed away, which left my sister, Heather, in need of extra help for schooling. After a family meeting, we decided to partner with my dad and Heather to help her through her high school years.

As long as everything went smoothly, I was able to keep everything moving forward. If any glitch occurred, however, disruptions became enormous. One rainy day as I rushed from one place to another, I realized (while at the gas station) that I did not have my credit card in my purse.

I hurried home "son in tow" and tried to enter our house through the garage but ran smack into the door, which was locked from the inside. I did not have a key to this door, so I had to run out in the rain, unlock the front door, and search the house for my misplaced card.

Before I could leave to run back out into the rain, something snapped inside me. I began kicking and screaming at the door.

A little voice behind me said, "Mommy, where's Jesus?"

Immediately, I saw Jesus (in my mind) reaching under my car seat, smiling, and picking up my credit card. Sure enough, when I huffed over to my car, my credit card was right there where Jesus showed me.

Tim's ability to interject truth in the midst of my temper tantrum helped to dissipate my rage. He used a tool I often employed with my kids to help them sort through their emotions. Tim's response to my rage worked because we had cultivated a family value to submit ourselves to God.

Family members who are able to support each other in shifting atmospheres "do life" well together. When biblical values are taught as normal aspects for the family, each member, including children, becomes a powerful carrier of heaven's atmospheres.

NOTES

1. Blue Letter Bible, s.v. "Radah," accessed January 2, 2017, https://www.blueletterbible.org/lang/lexicon/lexicon.cfm?Strongs=H7287&t=ESV.

2. Ibid., s.v. "Kēryssō," accessed February 10, 2017, https://www.blueletterbible.org/lang/lexicon/lexicon.cfm?Strongs=G2784&t=ESV.

3. "The World's Tallest Man", https://shop.bethel.com/collections/prosperous-soul/products/the-world-s-tallest-man.

CHAPTER ELEVEN

SHIFTING ATMOSPHERES OVER REGIONS

To me, though I am the very least of all the saints,
this grace was given, to preach to the Gentiles
the unsearchable riches of Christ, and to bring
to light for everyone what is the plan of the
mystery hidden for ages in God, who created all
things, so that through the church the manifold
wisdom of God might now be made known to the
rulers and authorities in the heavenly places.
—EPHESIANS 3:8-10

As we venture into our understanding of regional atmospheres, it is important we outline the higher beings belonging to

Satan's kingdom. These are the spiritual beings residing in the *heavenly places* that hold influence over our natural world. Though these, too, can be referred to as demons, they hold much more influence than the average unclean spirit and tend to operate at a higher level—meaning they work to exercise control over key regions, nations, and people to complete specific tasks for the enemy. Depending on your Bible's translation, these evil spirits are listed as *principalities (rulers)*, *powers (authorities)*, and *rulers over the darkness of this world (cosmic powers)*.

In *The Three Battlegrounds*, Francis Frangipane describes *principalities (rulers)* as a high class of spirit-beings in the satanic hierarchy. The word *principality* (or *ruler*, in the ESV) means the first place, rule, or magistracy of angels and demons. As higher beings in Satan's government, principalities serve to implement hell's anti-Christ agendas in human society. We can see this because the word *magistrate*, chosen by the original author to define "principality," means a civil officer who administers the law.

These are the unclean spirits who receive orders from the upper echelons of darkness and pass them on to lower-ranking demons. These lesser demons represent the common "foot soldiers" of hell—identified frequently in Scripture as unclean spirits. Principalities are not as high-ranking as powers and world rulers but nevertheless serve a critical aspect of the devil's kingdom.

Powers or *authorities*, depending on your translation, are defined as "the power of rule or government." Placed above principalities but beneath *world rulers of darkness (cosmic powers)*, *powers* serve as the administration of hell's government. These are the entities that issue/manage Satan's commands. Powers receive the devil's orders and delegate to principalities, who then dictate them to hell's lower ranks. *Powers* serve as the system by which Satan's kingdom is operated. With the father of lies at the top, his slaves and fellow beings work to implement all sorts of wickedness.

World or *cosmic rulers* serve as elite beings placed in authority over entire nations and global regions. These are the spirits revealed to Daniel when he interceded for the freedom of his people. Visited by God's messenger, the Hebrew was told of the reason for his prayer's delay; it was not due to anything he lacked or did incorrectly but to the magnitude of the spiritual battle that surrounded him:

> *Then he* [the angel] *said to me, "Fear not, Daniel, for from the first day that you set your heart to understand and humbled yourself before your God, your words have been heard, and I have come because of your words. The prince of the kingdom of Persia withstood me twenty-one days, but Michael, one of the chief princes, came to help me, for I was left there with the kings of Persia, and came to make you understand what is to happen to your people in the latter days. For the vision is for days yet to come"* (Daniel 10:12-14).

In this passage, the Lord's angel revealed an interesting truth about spiritual warfare—when it comes to the angelic and demonic realm, there appears to be a hierarchical authority. Although the messenger angel was dispatched, an evil spirit with more authority (due to hierarchy) withstood the deliverance until an even greater angel, Michael, was released.

When it comes to dealing with *principalities*, *powers*, and *world rulers*, our most effective method of warfare is to displace their authority rather than directly cast them out. Displacement occurs when we exercise our weapons of warfare referenced in Chapter Four. Notice that Daniel did not engage with the world ruler himself. Instead, he left the battle to God and was protected under His covering. Daniel's contribution to the fight, rather than confront the elite spirit head on, was to devote himself to a period of intense prayer and fasting:

> *In those days I, Daniel, was mourning for three weeks.*
> *I ate no delicacies, no meat or wine entered my mouth,*
> *nor did I anoint myself at all, for the full three weeks*
> (Daniel 10:2-3).

I write this because when it comes to dealing with powers, principalities, and world rulers (and you could argue in all spiritual warfare), the battle belongs to God. We should never search out demons to attack; our focus should be on expanding the Lord's Kingdom. If we focus too much on battling the enemy, we will wear ourselves out. We must, instead, assume an intercessory stance like Daniel and partner with God as He releases His angelic army to destroy the works of darkness.

> OUR MOST EFFECTIVE METHOD OF WARFARE IS TO DISPLACE THEIR AUTHORITY RATHER THAN DIRECTLY CAST THEM OUT.

In Daniel's case, the Lord dispatched Michael to bring authority over the prince of Persia. He did not have Daniel engage with it himself. God did not delegate this authority to Daniel; instead, Daniel stood in the gap for his people and prayed. As we work to reverse the enemy's hold over our nations, cities, and regions, our main weapon of warfare is intercession. These higher evil beings may not be cast out because they are working through multiple people in the region. They must instead be displaced:

> The means through which the church successfully wars against principalities [and powers and rulers] is through Christ's spiritual authority and the principle of displacement. Principalities are not "cast out," for they do not dwell in people; they dwell in "heavenly places." They are displaced in the spirit-realm by the ascendancy of Christ in the church and, through the church, into community.[1]

The church can re-terraform the earth to line up with the Lord's will through acts of intercession, partnership with Christ's authority, and outreach to our communities with practical godly trainings and hands-on help.

We sometimes perceive intercession as an elite form of prayer—something that only high-ranking prayer warriors or little old ladies can participate in. In truth, the Bible encourages all Christians to intercede. We can define the word *intercession* as "the action of intervening or of saying a prayer on behalf of another person." Put simply, intercession is our way of covering one another. All Christians can exercise this gift no matter their experience or leadership position. If we examine Jesus, we see that He was the ultimate example of a powerful intercessor. Even at the point of His death, He continued to beseech the Father to forgive humanity (see Luke 23:34).

Even the Holy Spirit engages in intercession. Paul writes:

> *Likewise the Spirit helps us in our weakness. For we do not know what to pray for as we ought, but the Spirit himself intercedes for us with groanings too deep for words* (Romans 8:26).

Similar to Daniel's experience, the Holy Spirit serves as an intense intercessor. Whereas Daniel prayed and fasted so hard that he mourned for several weeks, the Holy Spirit (on a much larger scale) utters deep *groans* or *sighs* on our behalf.

This might make intercession seem a heavy or undesired gift. Make no mistake, intercession, though powerful, does not have to wear us down. Beni Johnson does a great job of addressing this in her book *The Happy Intercessor,* in which she dispels the myth that all intercessors must be depressed and constantly under attack. Instead, she encourages intercessors to align themselves with joy in their dependence on God. Doing so protects us from the weariness that sometimes attaches to us in seasons of warfare.

Stacy was a young believer who carried a passion for prayer and justice. Growing up, her dad had been an alcoholic who verbally abused her and her two youngest sisters. Now in their own marriages, Stacy began to see common patterns of rage developing in the households of her siblings.

Stacy took ownership over atmospheres in their homes and repented on behalf of her sisters who had partnered with her father's sins. Standing in the gap for their situations, Stacy prayed, "Holy Spirit, please forgive me and any members of my family who have partnered with rage. I ask you to forgive us in Jesus's name and to release peace in place of rage."

Miraculously, the verbal fights her sisters experienced with their husbands decreased in frequency. Stacy began to notice a pervading feeling of God's presence that outweighed the previous atmospheres of anger, bitterness, fear, and rage.

Interestingly, Stacy never felt "oppressed" or "discouraged" while she interceded for her sisters because she did not allow these issues they were dealing with to take ownership over her life. This is a great example of healthy intercession. When God prompts us to pray and we lean into discernment, intercession can be an encouragement to our hearts.

A similar pattern emerges when we intercede for our cities, nations, and regions. This type of intercession comes from Second Chronicles:

> If my people who are called by my name humble themselves, and pray and seek my face and turn from their wicked ways, then I will hear from heaven and will forgive their sin and heal their land (2 Chronicles 7:14).

Prayers like this keep you in alignment and covered by Jesus as you intercede for your community. Here is an example:

Humbling yourself:

> Father God, I ask You to forgive me for any way I have partnered with the spirit of (insert name of spirit here) over my city (or region).

Turning from wicked ways:

> *I forgive the people in my region who have agreed with this spirit and have given it a place to dwell. I ask You, Holy Spirit, to turn the hearts of the people back to Father God so that You can begin to teach us how to live godly lives.*

Receiving healing:

> *Jesus, I ask that You would displace the spirit of (insert the name of the spirit here) and replace with Your Father's opposite (insert what God wants to release).*

When we take the time to hear what the Lord wishes to impart, He will release the fullness of His blessing. Sometimes, what the Lord releases is not an obvious opposite, so we need to be willing to hear His voice.

> WHEN GOD PROMPTS US TO PRAY AND WE LEAN INTO DISCERNMENT, INTERCESSION CAN BE AN ENCOURAGEMENT TO OUR HEARTS.

One night, I had a horrible dream that included a theme of incest in it. I woke up very distressed because I knew that what I had picked up was in the atmosphere around me. I called my good friend, Renee, and we went to lunch. She admitted that she, too, had picked up this demonic broadcast.

I was quite angry at the enemy and my justice meter kicked into high gear. I declared into the atmosphere, "Not on my watch! Get your filthy hands off the children."

This in itself was not a wrong prayer, but my anger veiled a deeper strategy from the enemy. When I discussed this with a prophet friend, Ben Armstrong, he asked, "Did you ask God to release an atmosphere of proper intimacy among families?"

No, I thought. *Had not even crossed my mind.* I was so on guard against the enemy's plans that I did not stop to think about what God wanted to release in its place.

As we discuss principalities, powers, and rulers, be comforted in the fact that it does not matter how specific you are in identifying its authority. For instance, when I go into a city and discern its atmospheres, I do not ask the Lord what sort of principalities or powers are ruling the environment. All I care about is the agenda or message these principalities and powers are broadcasting and seeding into the environment. If a city suffers under a spirit of suicide, it does not matter to me if this emanates from a world ruler, principality, or power. All I care about is reversing the devil's work, renouncing partnership with it and asking God to release His broadcast in its place.

We should not constantly search for the principalities and powers; they are not ours to engage. God will send his angels to do the heavy lifting as long as we humble ourselves and partner with how He wants us to pray. It is our job to provide support to His army through worship, praise, prophetic and scriptural declarations, acts of love, and intercession. We are God's "terraformers" who partner with Him to reclaim the earth's territory for His reign. Our job is to cleanse the atmosphere; God's job is to cast down the heavenly beings that rule these areas.

———◆———

Many times, God will have us perform prophetic acts instead of actually engaging the enemy. Prophetic acts can be a lot of fun and sometimes a bit strange. My prophetic intercessor friends have repeatedly told me what God has asked them to do to shift regional atmospheres. Sometimes, God has asked them to take bread and cast it out onto a body of water. Other times, He has told them to take wine and pour it over a rock. Although we do not know what these acts of obedience accomplish, our simple acts of obedience open doors to the angelic.

> GOD WILL SEND HIS ANGELS TO DO THE HEAVY LIFTING AS LONG AS WE HUMBLE OURSELVES AND PARTNER WITH HOW HE WANTS US TO PRAY.

Another way we can displace powers, principalities, and world rulers is to step past the four walls of the church and engage in community outreach. No city, nation, or region is truly free apart from God's church sowing into the community. God's people have a mandate to go outside the church and reveal the Kingdom of Heaven, for example, by feeding the poor, building businesses, and interceding for government officials. I feel compelled to repeat this verse from a previous chapter:

> *You are the light of the world. A city set on a hill cannot be hidden. Nor do people light a lamp and put it under a basket, but on a stand, and it gives light to all in the house. In the same way, let your light shine before others, so that they may see your good works and give glory to your Father who is in heaven* (Matthew 5:14-16).

In Western society, we tend to think of *good works* as acts solely associated with benevolence or caregiving. While acts are extremely valuable, they are not the only ways we can displace the enemy's kingdom.

The phrase *good works* have several translations that include businesses, employments, enterprises, any products whatsoever, anything accomplished by hand, arts, industries, minds, acts, deeds, or things done. According to the Bible, when we build businesses, serve our employers, create products and works of art, and do good deeds, we are pointing people to our Father.

As we accept our calling as stewards of this planet and we begin to shift atmospheres, we will see the kingdoms of this world become the kingdoms of our God (see Rev. 11:15).

NOTE

1. Francis Frangipane, *The Three Battlegrounds* (Cedar Rapids, IA: Arrow Publications, 2006) Kindle loc. 1273.

CHAPTER TWELVE

ASSIGNMENTS

December 19, 2010
by Cory De Silva

Death sat on the freeway's side
and watched me—impatient, anxious,
and annoyed. Chewing his fingernails
as I climbed from the shattered windshield
of my car. Held his breath as I collapsed
on concrete, hummingbird holes punched
into my skin like art, leaking red
onto a canvas of rain-stained
pavement. Rose from his seat
to collect me as firefighters crowded,
ambulances arrived, and angels stood guard.
He could not get close enough to take me.
Repressed and dissatisfied, Death packed
his scythe and left. A coffin-shaped hat
tipping in the wind. Bony fingers
pulling the edges of his cloak
closer to the emptiness of his face.

Six months had passed since Cory's visit with the demonic spirit in our living room. While attending one of the late Sunday night services, my husband, Stephen, received a text message—Cory had been in a serious car accident on his way home from Southern California. His truck had hydroplaned in severe rain and careened into the interstate barrier at more than sixty miles an hour.

By God's grace, Cory had emerged from the crash relatively unscathed. The only mark from the accident was a light welt on his neck caused by the seat belt. The on-site police officer, having surveyed the wreck, shook his head and said, "I don't know how you made it. I was out here two days ago with the same kind of accident and two people were decapitated."

Steve and I thanked the Lord for Cory's protection. Days later, we drove down for a visit. Boasting a totaled car and a pronounced seat-belt burn, Cory recounted the story of his near-death experience.

"One minute I was swerving. The next I was upside down begging God not to let me die."

Acknowledging God's protection, we celebrated the obvious testimony and shared it with our friends. Cory even wrote a poem, which begins this chapter, and shared it with his university creative writing class.

While we visited with Cory, we learned of several other instances when Cory had been miraculously saved in driving-related accidents. In another occurrence, Cory had stopped at a four-way intersection on his way to school. Out of nowhere, a rusty truck ran a red light and swerved psychotically toward him.

Cory glanced up to see the oncoming vehicle. To his left stood a guard rail. To his right, a semi. In less than five seconds, he and the truck would collide—the other vehicle swerving at a speed of fifty miles per hour. At the last second, the truck veered into oncoming traffic and disappeared amidst an angry squawk of horns and squealing tires. Once again, God had intervened and spared the life of our son.

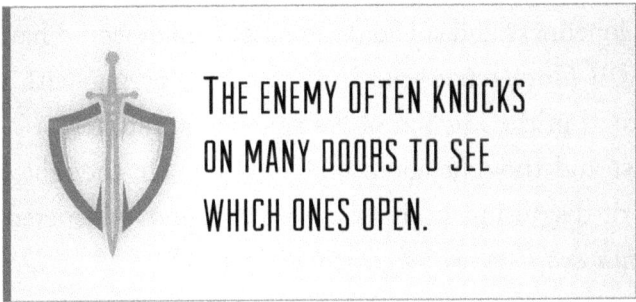

> # THE ENEMY OFTEN KNOCKS ON MANY DOORS TO SEE WHICH ONES OPEN.

It seemed to us a demonic assignment had been sent to halt or slow our son's destiny. This assignment, starting with a tactic of fear, began with an evil spirit appearing to Cory in our living room. This attempt, made to create insecurity in Cory's relationship with God, was cut short because of his confidence in Christ. The demon's first tactic did not work. When Cory renounced its presence, the unclean spirit was forced to flee.

This lack of fear gave Cory authority at that moment over the assigned spirit. Although it vanished, we later found out that the assignment was still in play. Instead of continuing to confront him openly (because that did not work), the demon resorted to a more covert form of warfare—continuous "I" messages in the form of suicidal thoughts.

Having struggled with loneliness and insignificance throughout his life (which were lies), Cory was a susceptible target of these attacks. The demons tested these thoughts and, having seen them take root in Cory's mind, moved forward to cut his life short. Notice that—while fear and intimidation did not work, hopelessness and self-hatred did. The enemy often knocks on many doors to see which ones open.

The spirits of hopelessness and suicide devised a new strategy and tag-teamed to destroy him. Eventually, these thoughts broke through and wore down his confidence. After months of intense loneliness and suicidal thoughts (which would have been defeated if Cory renounced instead of partnering with them), Cory stood in the kitchen of his apartment and held a knife to his wrist and thought about ending it all. He thought (or the evil spirit disguising itself as Cory's thoughts whispered), *why don't I just end it now and get rid of the pain?*

Thankfully, God's voice was prompting Cory as well. Other thoughts entered his mind like, *wait a second. That would be stupid. I have so many dreams to fulfill. Why the heck would I stop short of my dreams now?* Renouncing ties with this suicidal spirit, Cory returned the knife to its drawer and renounced the enemy's taunts.

Now the enemy's attempts had been thwarted twice. In a mixture of fear and desperation, the spirits decided to ratchet up their game and try to take Cory's life another way. They could not get him to partner with their thoughts any longer, so they needed a more drastic plan to eliminate him. Thus began the bizarre near-encounters with death that accumulated over the next few months.

After Cory's severe crash, we prayed for this assignment to be broken and the spiritual attacks stopped. Although the spirits succeeded in wrecking his car, they failed to actually harm him. Though they had been assigned by higher forces to take his life, God had sent His angels for protection. If we had known about the earlier attacks, we could have intervened in corporate prayer before his car crash. Either way, Steve and I remain grateful to this day for our son's protection.

Assignments are not fun to talk about. Who, after all, wants to hear about demons targeting them? If we embrace a victorious mindset, we can stand up against this knowledge and rest in the comfort of the Lord's protection. None of us truly knows how much God protects us on a daily basis, but Scripture reassures us that He does:

> *But the Lord is faithful. He will establish you and guard you against the evil one* (2 Thessalonians 3:3).

> *Be strong and courageous. Do not fear or be in dread of them, for it is the Lord your God who goes with you. He will not leave you or forsake you* (Deuteronomy 31:6).

> *God is our refuge and strength, a very present help in trouble* (Psalm 46:1).

If you find yourself in the midst of an attack or the target of an assignment, search Scripture and meditate on its promises of protection. Our pastor encourages us to read the promises and encouraging words we have received in the past because doing so takes our focus off of our trials and places it on God's promises for us.

> WHEN WE STAND IN THE
> CONFIDENCE OF THE BLOOD
> OF CHRIST, THE DEVIL IS
> FORCED TO LEAVE.

The best way to defend against an assignment is to partner with the sacrificial blood of Jesus. The shield that covers a multitude of sins, Christ's sacrifice, is our greatest refuge. The worst thing we can do when under an attack is to be afraid and partner with it. Christ is far more powerful than any spirit that raises itself against us. As we gird our hearts in the promises of God, His blood protects us:

> *Therefore, brothers, since we have confidence to enter the holy places by the blood of Jesus...let us draw near with a true heart in full assurance of faith, with our hearts sprinkled clean from an evil conscience and our bodies washed with pure water* (Hebrews 10:19,22).

> *But he was pierced for our transgressions; he was crushed for our iniquities; upon him was the chastisement that brought us peace, and with his wounds we are healed* (Isaiah 53:5).

> *And they have conquered him by the blood of the Lamb and by the word of their testimony, for they loved not their lives even unto death* (Revelation 12:11).

Intercession once again comes into bold relief as we apply the Lord's sacrifice to our lives. As the eternal mediator who intercedes on our behalf, Jesus's blood prevents destruction. A sign was given to us in Exodus when the obedient people of Israel were passed over by *the destroyer*, a spirit sent by God to execute judgment on Egypt:

> *Take a bunch of hyssop and dip it in the blood that is in the basin, and touch the lintel and the two door-posts with the blood that is in the basin. None of you shall go out of the door of his house until the morning. For the Lord will pass through to strike the Egyptians, and when he sees the blood on the lintel and on the two doorposts, the Lord will pass over the door and will not allow the destroyer to enter your houses to strike you* (Exodus 12:22-23).

Protected under the authority of the lamb's blood, the Hebrews were spared from destruction. This works with us today in our contemporary lives. As we cover ourselves with the blood of Jesus, the sacrificial love of God, the devil and his armies are forced to pass over. It is as though we wear an invisible cloak or impenetrable armor. When we stand in the confidence of the blood of Christ, the devil is forced to leave:

> *Submit yourselves therefore to God. Resist the devil, and he will flee from you* (James 4:7).

Several years ago, my family and I attended a wedding. Everyone looked happy and seemed to be enjoying themselves. That is, almost everyone. One of my family members, Dana (name changed), had suffered a brain aneurysm years before. Her body never fully recovered. As she limped past, I could not help but watch with sadness and think, *I can't believe this. I feel so bad for her.* Right then, a demonic spirit manifested itself, left Dana, and came directly at me. It said, *I'm coming for you!* Shocked, I jumped back and said, "You will not, in Jesus's name!"

I made it through the rest of the wedding, a bit shaken, but continued to praise the Lord and remind myself that He was bigger. I knew God did not give me a spirit of fear, so I began to speak truth over myself about God's protection and mercy.

A week later, my nose began to bleed. I had only experienced a bloody nose once before in my life so I was alarmed to see the amount blood gushing out for no apparent reason. As I jammed tissue up my nose, I heard the enemy's voice say, *See? I told you I was coming.*

I had a choice then to either partner with fear or to hand the battle over to Jesus. Fortunately, I chose the latter. I took the enemy's taunts captive and stewarded an internal atmosphere of peace.

Prompted by the Holy Spirit, I heard myself say out loud, "Thank You, Jesus, that this blood is coming out of my nose and not leaking into my brain." Over the next few days, my nose continued to randomly bleed. Every time, I thanked the Lord and said, "Thank You, Jesus, that the blood is draining out of my nose and not flooding into my brain."

A few weeks later, I learned that a friend of mine had been experiencing problems with her coordination and eyesight. The doctors finally diagnosed that she had been experiencing blood leaks in her brain. From then on, I acted as an intercessor. Whenever my nose began to bleed, I thanked God that it was not collecting in my brain and prayed that the bleeding would stop in hers.

My nosebleeds continued and my friend got worse. Finally, they placed her in intensive care. I continued to intercede for her and told the enemy, *You cannot have her.* Her son spent several nights in the ICU room with her and prayed for God to work a miracle. In the spirit, he saw a very large, dark figure fighting angels over his mother's body. I am sure that it was the same spirit that confronted me at the wedding.

Hours into another very long night, my friend's son felt a release in the spirit realm and his mom began to improve. The day she finally got her "all clear" sign from the doctor was the same day my nose bleeding stopped. Since then, I have not had another nose bleed. (That is until the day after I wrote about it in this book.)

Since then, I have reminded myself and the enemy that he has no right to harass me even when my nose begins to bleed. Even though I spent the next few weeks inconvenienced by this attack, the enemy was unable to release fear into my life.

WE MUST NOT ONLY REFUSE TO GIVE IN TO FEAR BUT ALSO STAND IN THE GAP FOR OTHERS THROUGH INTERCESSION SO THAT THE ENEMY HAS NO ONE TO ATTACK.

In this example, my friend and I both experienced a demonic assignment. These are different from the normal spiritual attacks that target your mind or the broadcasts that the enemy releases into the atmosphere. Although you will need to fight the thoughts (lies) that attack your mind, should you become a target of an assignment you will need an additional strategy to fight against it. The Bible depicts an assignment as a lion wanting to devour you:

> *Be sober-minded; be watchful. Your adversary the devil prowls around like a roaring lion, seeking someone to devour* (1 Peter 5:8).

His first assault may be to roar at you and scare you into opening a door of fear. If that does not work, he may simply skip over you and seek someone else to devour. We must not only refuse to give in to fear but also stand in the gap for others through intercession so that the enemy has no one to attack.

Jesus was the perfect example of how one navigates spiritual battle. Because Jesus had such confidence in His life calling and a strong relationship with His Father, there was literally no way the enemy could wage successful warfare against Him.

If you find yourself or a loved one in the midst of a demonic assignment, partner with God to plead the blood of Jesus over your life. Repent for any fear you have allowed into your life and meditate on the Scriptures that reveal the power of God. Do not underestimate the power of Christ's blood. A few verses that will encourage you when faced with an attack are listed below:

For you have died, and your life is hidden with Christ in God (Colossians 3:3).

Keep me as the apple of your eye; hide me in the shadow of your wings (Psalm 17:8).

O Lord, in your strength the king rejoices, and in your salvation how greatly he exults! You have given him his heart's desire and have not withheld the request of his lips. For you meet him with rich blessings; you set a crown of fine gold upon his head. He asked life of you; you gave it to him, length of days forever and ever. His glory is great through your salvation; splendor and majesty you bestow on him. For you make him most blessed forever; you make him glad with the joy of your presence. For the king trusts in the Lord, and through the steadfast love of the Most High he shall not be moved.

Your hand will find out all your enemies; your right hand will find out those who hate you. You will make them as a blazing oven when you appear. The Lord will swallow them up in his wrath, and fire will consume them. You will destroy their descendants from the earth, and their offspring from among the children of man. Though they plan evil against you, though they devise mischief, they will not succeed. For you will put them to flight; you will aim at their face with your bows.

Be exalted, O Lord, in your strength! We will sing and praise your power (Psalm 21).

FINAL THOUGHTS

Have you not known? Have you not heard? The Lord is the everlasting God, the Creator of the ends of the earth. He does not faint or grow weary; his understanding is unsearchable. He gives power to the faint, and to him who has no might he increases strength. Even youths shall faint and be weary, and young men shall fall exhausted; but they who wait for the Lord shall renew their strength; they shall mount up with wings like eagles; they shall run and not be weary; they shall walk and not faint.
—ISAIAH 40:28-31

The Bible promises those who wait on the Lord will be victorious. Like the man who builds his house on rocks, so we who build a strong relationship with God will remain steadfast in the midst of struggle and storms. There is truly only one weapon when it comes to standing above the spiritual realm and that is an intimate relationship with the Persons of the Trinity—Father God, Jesus, and the Holy Spirit. Even Jesus needed a relationship with the Father. If He needed it, how much more do we?

> *Therefore Jesus answered and was saying to them, "Truly, truly, I say to you, the Son can do nothing of Himself, unless it is something He sees the Father doing; for whatever the Father does, these things the Son also does in like manner* (John 5:19 NASB).

All of Satan's authority was crushed under the weight of Jesus's blood. We have a fresh start—a summons. We are part of God's army and are set by God on the front lines to charge forward and retake the world's atmospheres. If you use the principles presented in this book, I am confident you will succeed. Begin small. Start by shifting your own atmospheres. Find your normal and get rid of any bad trees in your garden. Lean into the Holy Spirit to gain insight and strategies as you practice discernment of the spiritual world around you. Most of all, dive into the Word of God. You will find your peace and courage there:

> *Whatever you ask in my name, this I will do, that the Father may be glorified in the Son. If you ask me anything in my name, I will do it* (John 14:13-14).

> *Fear not, for I am with you; be not dismayed, for I am your God; I will strengthen you, I will help you, I will uphold you with my righteous hand. Behold, all who are incensed against you shall be put to shame*

and confounded; those who strive against you shall be as nothing and shall perish. You shall seek those who contend with you, but you shall not find them; those who war against you shall be as nothing at all. For I, the Lord your God, hold your right hand; it is I who say to you, "Fear not, I am the one who helps you" (Isaiah 41:10-13).

And Jesus answered them, "Truly, I say to you, if you have faith and do not doubt, you will not only do what has been done to the fig tree, but even if you say to this mountain, 'Be taken up and thrown into the sea,' it will happen. And whatever you ask in prayer, you will receive, if you have faith" (Matthew 21:21-22).

If you abide in me, and my words abide in you, ask whatever you wish, and it will be done for you (John 15:7).

> EVEN JESUS NEEDED A RELATIONSHIP WITH THE FATHER. IF HE NEEDED IT, HOW MUCH MORE DO WE?

I bless you in your journey as you shift atmospheres and take back all ground stolen by the enemy in Jesus's precious name.

ABOUT
DAWNA DE SILVA

DAWNA DE SILVA and her husband Stephen have ministered out of Bethel Church in Redding, California for over twenty years preaching, speaking internationally, and authoring books. Whether training Sozo, preaching, shifting atmospheres, or ministering prophetically, Dawna releases people, churches, and cities into new vision and freedom. No matter how traumatic the wounding, Dawna ministers with authority and gentleness, imparting hope and healing.